Published by: Tellington TTouch Training - Canada - 2017
Revised 2019
Coldstream B.C.   www.ttouch.ca   ttouch@shaw.ca

Disclaimer of Liability
The authors and Tellington TTouch Training® shall have neither liability nor responsibility to any person or entity with respect to any loss or damage caused or alleged to be caused directly or indirectly by the information contained in this book. While the book is as accurate as the authors can make it, there may be errors, omissions and inaccuracies.

About the Authors:
Robyn Hood is the sister of Linda Tellington-Jones and a Senior Instructor for Tellington TTouch Training. When she is not travelling teaching TTouch, she lives near Vernon, BC with her husband and many four legged friends including a herd of about 50 Icelandic horses.

Mandy Pretty is Robyn's daughter and has been involved with the TTouch work since she was a child. She is a Tellington TTouch Instructor for horses and a Connected Riding Associate Instructor. She teaches workshops, does intensive individual work and is in charge of training at The Icelandic Horse Farm.

Other titles by the authors
All Wrapped Up for Horses - Robyn Hood with Mandy Pretty
All Wrapped Up for Pets - Robyn Hood with Mandy Pretty
All Wrapped Up for People - Robyn Hood with Mandy Pretty

Training & Retraining Horses - The Tellington Way - Linda Tellington Jones with Mandy Pretty

Cover Photo by Annalena Kuhn www.annalena-kuhn.de

Distributed in the UK by Cetacea Publishing www.cetaceapublishing.com Printed in the EU

Contents

Part 6

Part 7

Part 8

Part 9

Part 10

A note about this book

When I first thought about writing this booklet I thought it would be helpful for Tellington TTouch practitioners and those going through the program as a reminder to some of the different harnesses we use and how we use them. I thought it would be about 20 – 30 pages and show various configurations. Once it was started it became clear that we could include the various rope configurations for leading, such as the Beeline, Butterfly and Dragonfly that I started teaching more than 10 years ago and have been refining ever since.

The book is not so much a "dog training" book, as a "people training" book with the focus on how to make walking on a leash a more pleasant experience for both dogs and their people. We have included awareness exercises to help people change their posture which will improve their communication and effectiveness with their dogs. This is an approach to teaching that we always implement in our workshops - you "see it"; you "feel it"; you "do it" and you "teach it". Although people aren't dogs, just having a chance to walk in their paws, can help influence our understanding and approach.

Throughout I mention the importance of allowing dogs to use their noses to sniff and I suggest you look into finding some "nose work" activities with your dog. It is definitely one activity that dogs would sign up for and gives your dog a chance to really "read the newspaper" with their nose.

It is one thing to write about a concept and quite another to write directions for techniques that people may not be familiar with. The focus here is on many different exercises to help give dogs and people new and different experiences to do with walking on leash. We tried to convey the 'how to' with photos and text but you can see many of the techniques, step by step, on videos on our YouTube channel.

My daughter, Mandy Pretty, did the majority of the writing and I provided some ideas. It couldn't have been done without her.

I hope you find this booklet helpful.

Robyn Hood

This is the 2nd Edition with updates including the TTouch Connector. We took out the details on harnesses because there are so many suitable harnesses on the market.

$\mathbf{D}$ogs are amazing animals. Few other species live with us in such a cohesive, all encompassing way as part of the family.

The Tellington TTouch® Method is a complete system of working with animals that combines a holistic approach of gentle bodywork techniques, mindful ground work, leash exercises as well as a variety of equipment to support healthy posture. TTouch has long been associated with reducing anxiety in dogs, helping them get over fear and reactivity, and enhancing overall well being and trust. The combination of Tellington TTouch Bodywork, Groundwork and equipment works together to create new patterns of healthy posture and behavior, while maintaining and fostering a trusting and cooperative relationship with your dog. A fundamental part of the Method is "Change Your Mind, Change Your Dog" and "Change the Posture, Change the Behavior." These two concepts help foster positive, long term change without the use of force or punishment.

For more detailed information about the specific Tellington TTouch Bodywork techniques please refer to "Getting In TTouch with Your Dog", by Linda Tellington-Jones, the foundation text for using the Method with your dog. "Getting in TTouch with Your Dog", covers many leading exercises, use of harnesses and the Playground of Higher Learning.

Combining Tellington TTouch exercises and techniques, along with the TTouch philosophy, goes beyond basic training and helps to create long term, innate changes in the way your dog responds to you and his surroundings. Instead of simply looking at the basic, possibly unwanted behavior, we look for the root cause of that behavior and initiate change by addressing how the dog feels about his situation. For many dog owners, the most exasperating behavioral issues can be those seen when their dog is on leash. Traditionally pulling and/or reactivity would be addressed with a variety of aversive devices or techniques. While these can all work to change the behavior itself, they do not necessarily address the reason the dog was exhibiting the behavior in the first place.

Understanding the fundamental tenets behind the Tellington TTouch philosophy, utilizing equipment that helps dogs walk in better balance, and then implementing simple, yet effective, leading exercises combines to create a system that enables handlers to help their dogs find balance, self confidence and self control. Empowering our dogs to feel better in their own skin allows them to act better, creating positive habits and behavior at its deepest level.

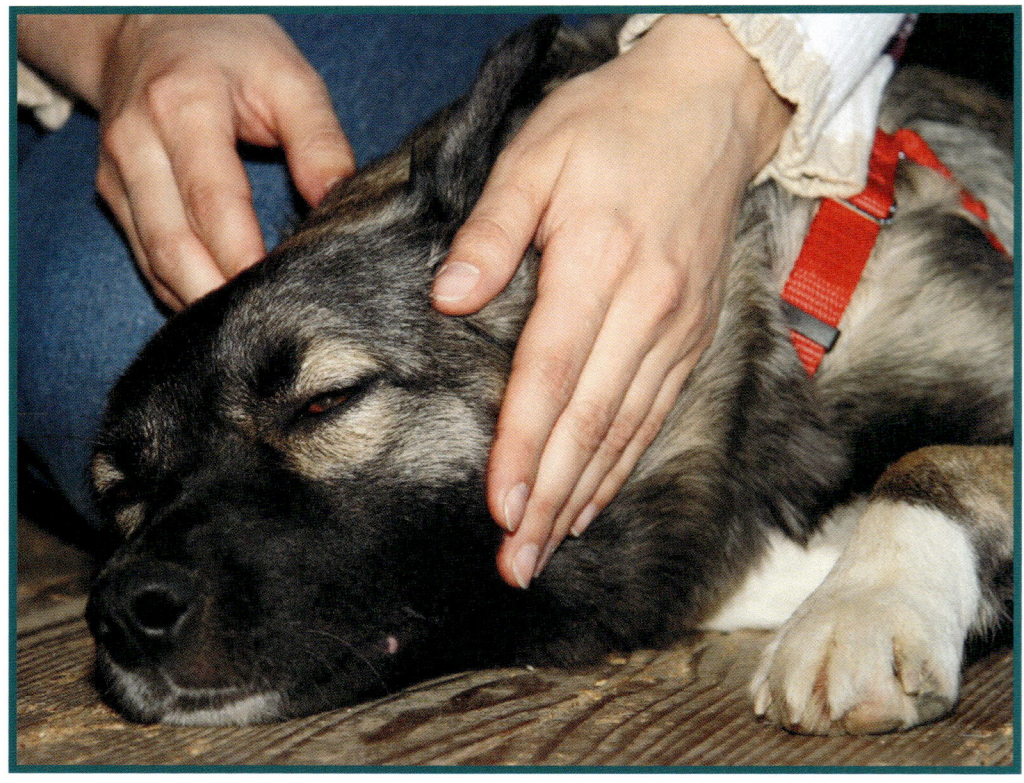

The Tellington TTouch Method incorporates observation, gentle bodywork techniques, mindful leading exercises and innovative and gentle equipment to help foster self-carriage (physical balance, boosting self-confidence (mental balance), which work together to help dogs have better self-control and make better choices (emotional balance).

Leash pulling; is there any other single issue that troubles dogs and their owners more? While it may be the owners who outwardly struggle with the issue, it is most certainly a detriment to the dogs as well.

The ideal scenario is that a dog walks on a loose leash cooperatively at all times; however, this is not the reality in the majority of cases. When confronted with this issue of leash pulling, it is not uncommon to hear it described as "my dog likes to pull on the leash" or "my dog only pulls when there is a distraction".

Dogs only pull when there is something to pull against, ie. the leash or more accurately, the human attached to the leash. While anxiety, excitement, fear or other emotions will intensify or trigger the pull in the first place, the leash is the point of issue. Let's face it; it's not our dog's fault that he pulls. It was our idea to put the dog on the tether. It's up to us to change how we use it.

This booklet will help you with tips and techniques to make it easier for us (and our dogs) to have a better experience on your daily walk or anytime they are on a leash.

In later discussions we will explore why this impasse of dog and handler pulling occurs and how we can help our dogs to adjust their balance by meeting the pull and melting. Moving forward in relation to the dog, changing the pressure on the collar or harness, exercises to check yourself and many equipment options are all here to help you find the best solution for you and your dog. We hope you enjoy discovering different ways to walk with your dog and **both** have fun on your forays into the great outdoors.

Opposition Response?

So what is the Opposition Response? In short, it's physics. For every action there is an equal and opposite reaction. We all have an innate response to pull back when we feel pressure.

When we respond to a tug on the leash with equal pressure we engage in the cycle of pulling. Since it was our idea to put a leash on a dog, it is up to us to consciously break this cycle and resist the base response to simply pull back, it is a learned response to give and that goes for us and our animals too.

Physics 101

We have established that dogs that pull only do so when on leash, but why is that? The simple answer is physics. Newton's Third Law of Physics states; "For every action, there is an equal and opposite reaction." This 'opposition reflex' that triggers dogs to pull is why dogs only pull when on leash, without anything (or anyone) to pull against. When dogs pull forward most humans, reflexively, go into a counter balance pull, to avoid falling over, stop the dog's trajectory or as a 'correction' on the neck to stop the forward movement. All of these instinctive reactions tend to have the opposite effect we are looking for.

If dogs did not have anything to pull against, leash pulling would not exist; we, as the handlers, are the equal and opposite force in the reaction equation.

So why do some dogs pull on leash and others easily walk along on a loose leash? While there are a variety of complex reasons that can go into the leash pulling scenario, much of it comes back to a basic question of balance and self-carriage.

Being in self-carriage allows an animal to better adapt to new stimuli, physical or mental. Having self-carriage implies that the animal tends to have a functional, biomechanically correct posture that enables movement and reaction without requiring large adjustments of balance or prolonged moments in reflex.

A dog that is very unbalanced physically, mentally, and/or emotionally will tend to be out of balance in all of these areas. This is well displayed in many dogs that are 'dog reactive" on leash. Often these same dogs are not at all "dog reactive" when off leash, which suggests that it is the confinement of the leash that triggers this response.

Hint Hound

Slower than Molasses?

While leash pulling gets all the limelight, many dogs have what seems to be the opposite problem, lagging or freezing.

In reality lagging on lead is actually the same problem as pulling, just in the opposite direction. Many dogs that lag, especially puppies, have just never really been taught how to walk on leash; they have just been dragged along. For many dogs this is very stressful and may put them into a "Freeze" response, creating even more lag, making for a very frustrating relationship for dog AND handler.

To help change the way a lagging dog feels about walking on leash, refer to the Harmony Handle (Page 23) and the Bee Line (page 43). These techniques use a sliding connection to the leash rather than a fixed one, which gives the dog a better sense of freedom and ease of movement.

Most dogs who lag become more engaged and responsive on leash once they find their own balance and are given the chance to be on lead without being pulled or dragged.

A Pain in the Neck

One of the biggest triggers for leash pulling can be the collar. This is contrary to the popular but out dated belief that harnesses will "make" your dog pull.

Some harnesses are meant to encourage your dog to pull, as is the case with a sled dog harness or a tracking harness; the further back the point of contact with the leash, the more it encourages the dog to pull.

The opposite is also true – the further forward the point of contact with the leash, the less it encourages pulling. The challenge with having just one point of contact on the front is that often restricts shoulder movement and pulls into the off-side. Any piece of equipment can encourage pulling if there is pressure on the leash.

Pressure on the collar can have physiological and postural implications that are far reaching and usually make the overall cycle of pulling more extreme.

Just imagine wearing a collar with an external force pulling on you; or worse yet, a choke collar that is pulling and tightening like a noose around your neck. Rather than make you feel safe, or like you had any control in the situation, it is more likely to create tension or increased anxiety.

For many dogs pressure on the collar does seem to increase anxiety, reactivity and arousal levels. There are several reasons for this:

First: The single point of contact on a collar can have a "fish on the end of the line effect" as a dog fidgets and fights to move away or towards an object of concern or interest. With only one point of leash connection there is very little influence on the dog's body. The handler can only limit the distance of travel.

Second: The placement of the collar on most dogs means that any pressure will lift their heads, drop their backs and effectively place more weight onto their front legs, or forehand. This is an excellent way to trigger the "opposition reflex" which causes dogs to pull in the first place.

On the Forehand?

Unless you happen to be a horse person, this term may seem foreign. While it is traditionally a horse term, "on the forehand" is a fantastic way to describe the way many dogs are perpetually out of balance.

When an animal is described as "on the forehand" it simply means that they have a disproportionate amount of weight on their front limbs, causing them to be out of balance. This imbalance may be imperceptible or be the cause of a myriad of undesirable behaviours' such as leash pulling and reactivity, and is hard on a dog's shoulders and hips.

Shifting a dogs balance from off the forehand will mean that they are not falling forward with gravity and do not tend to lead through their chest.

Third: The reason that collars can potentially cause an increased reaction in pulling and reactivity is a physiological one. Dr. Peter Dobias DVM, a veterinarian in Vancouver, British Columbia, states that collars can lead to "hypothyroidism, ear and eye problems, paw licking, Wobbler's Syndrome and general health deterioration." (see box) Physiological repercussions are also a very big reason

This is not to say that dogs cannot learn to walk politely on a loose leash and be okay on a flat collar, but the reality is that a dog who learns to walk politely in class, in a controlled setting, will not always be able to do so in the world outside the class setting.

There are many positive ways to teach good leash manners and obedience that encourage loose leash walking. Tellington TTouch goes beyond just training the behavior and considers the experience from the dog's perspective. Our hope is that you are able to take your dog for a walk, allow him some sniffing time and enjoy the experience without either of you pulling on the leash. The exercises and techniques outlined in this book will provide the foundations for enjoyable, enriching, and cooperative communication between you and your dog and can also be a supplement for any training you may choose to pursue.

A dog on leash does not have much choice in terms of where they can go or when they can leave a potentially stressful situation. If a dog is nervous or fearful of other dogs, and is not in control of where he can go, it is not surprising that he may have an "I'll get you before you get me" response. This starts the cycle of pulling on the leash, the handler in turns stops the forward motion, giving the dog something to pull against. When dogs are in better balance physically, with their weight equally over all four feet instead of leaning forward and find self-carriage, they feel safer (have more self-confidence) and can act instead of react (make better choices). This is the philosophical basis for all of the Tellington TTouch exercises.

A handler working with their dog on a harness, ideally with two points of contact, will be better equipped to rebalance and redirect their dog, without adding stress and pressure to an already aroused or anxious dog.

Basics of Balance

One of the most important tenets at the heart of the Tellington TTouch Method is the intrinsic relationship between physical, mental and emotional balance.

Virtually all behavioral issues encountered by handlers can be improved by enhancing physical balance. As dogs find their physical balance and find **SELF CARRIAGE**, they feel safer and become more **SELF CONFIDENT**. An animal who has more self confidence is more likely to act rather than react because they have more **SELF CONTROL**, giving them the opportunity to **MAKE BETTER CHOICES** in any situation they encounter.

ONE "JERK" CAN CAUSE A LOT OF DAMAGE

Dr. Peter Dobias DVM ~ www.peterdobias.com

Why is that? The neck and cervical spine are one of the most important energy channels in the body. If the flow of energy between the head and the neck is interrupted or restricted, a whole array of problems may arise, from lameness to skin problems, allergies and even cancer.

Hypothyroidism (low thyroid gland hormone)

For the longest time, I have been puzzled about why dogs known to pull on the leash, such as Labradors, Retrievers and German Shepherds, have such a high rates of thyroid gland issues. One day it dawned on me that the collar pushes on the throat exactly in the area of the thyroid gland. This gland gets severely traumatized whenever a dog pulls on the leash.

The thyroid gland gets inflamed and consequently 'destroyed' by the body's own immune system that tries to remove the inflamed thyroid cells. The destruction of the thyroid gland cells leads to the deficit of thyroid hormone – or hypothyroidism.

The thyroid gland governs the metabolism of every cell and its absence can have very severe consequences. The symptoms may be low energy, weight gain, skin problems, hair loss, a tendency for ear infections and organ failure to name a few.

Ear and eye issues

Eye and ear problems may also be related to pulling on the leash. Why? My experience is that pulling decreases the energy and lymphatic flow to the head, which leads to ear and eye conditions. My clients are often perplexed when all the ear and eye problems disappear after switching their dog from a collar to the right front clip harness.

Paw licking and foreleg lameness

This too can be related to your dog's collar. Pulling the leash often causes an abnormal sensation, or pins and needles, in the feet. Dogs try to lick their feet, not knowing what else to do. I have seen many so-called allergic dogs or chronically lame dogs healing completely after they were put on a special harness.

Some dogs may get such severe whiplash injuries from being jerked around that they suffer severe neck misalignment. A neck injury can pretty much affect any part of the body and if the energy flow deficit is severe, this can even predispose the individual to cancer.

"MOST PEOPLE DO NOT KNOW THAT LEASHES AND COLLARS CAN CAUSE SO MANY PROBLEMS"

Part 2 ~ Change Thyself

Regardless of what type of equipment you use to walk your dog; you as the walker have a huge amount of influence as to how the dog responds and how much you trigger the Opposition Response. A handler has three fundamental ways that they can easily change how effectively and positively they affect their dog; position relative to the dog, use of signals, and body posture.

Where do you stand?

The single easiest way to reduce the likelihood of pulling is to change where you stand in relation to your dog. The most effective position is level with your dog's neck. This means that you are ahead of, or at least even with, any point of contact attached to your dog. Ensuring that you stay level with your dog's head and neck will reduce how much you inadvertently create a backward pull on the leash, which sends the dog more forward and can trigger the Opposition Response.

If you close your eyes and imagine a person with a dog who pulls on the leash, what do you visualize? Most of us have an image of a dog forging forward and the handler being dragged along behind, much like a water skier.

Walking in a "water ski" position behind your dog, with pressure on the leash, is a surefire way to maintain pulling. Once you are behind you inadvertently feed the cycle of pull. One of the limitations with using very long training lines to teach a dog to walk on leash is that at such a distance you are unable to subtly rebalance and influence your dog. Thinking "up" rather than "back" when you give a signal is an important point to remember.

Hint Hound

Blame Game?

When a dog is labeled a "leash puller" the blame is usually placed on the dog. This means that the only choices are to add more correction, more distractions, more treats.

The reality is that the only thing we have complete control over is how **WE** respond to a situation. By acknowledging this you empower yourself to be the catalyst for change rather than placing all of the responsibility on the animal.

Using the 75 – 25 approach, the handler puts 75% of their attention on **HOW** they are asking and her own body position, and 25% to what the dog's response is.

By changing how we are asking our dog to do something, whether it is in our posture, technique or even intention, we will get more positive results faster and more effortlessly.

Swan Dive Exercise

When we walk at our dog's shoulder any pulling force is neutralized. As soon as a handler is back, they end up in a "Water Ski" position which feeds into the "Opposition Response" and puts the dog into an on the forehand, out of balance lean.

To feel how important it is to position yourself next to your dog's shoulder, try the simple Swan Dive Exercise for yourself.

Standing with your feet shoulder width apart, joints soft, put your arms out to the side. Notice that you are centered over the middle of your feet and that it feels easy to stand in balance.

Now, take you arms back so that they are behind your body, as they would look in a Swan Dive. What happened to your balance? Most people report that their weight shifts forward to counterbalance the arms and your weight is on the front of your feet and that it is very difficult not to take a step forward. This is exactly what happens to your dog as you lag behind and put pressure on the leash.

Now take your hands equally forward. Your balance shifted back. This is why it is important to stay ahead when using the Homing Pigeon (see page 46) or to avoid going into to a water skier position when you are leading your dog.

Balanced Alignment

Reorienting your position and changing your signals is much easier if you, the handler, are standing and walking in balance. Next time you are waiting somewhere in public, take a moment to notice the average posture of the passersby. Most people often stand with their shoulders and rib cage slightly behind the vertical (meaning their torso is leaning back slightly), so they are not stacked over their hips. This effectively tightens the lower back, locks the hips and knees which puts the person into an 'on the forehand', unbalanced posture.

When a handler is working in a braced, unbalanced posture it means that all of their signals will be more abrupt, less elastic, more mechanical and less comfortable for the person and the dog.

Taking the time to assess your own posture in the mirror can go a long way to improving body awareness and identifying what habits you tend to fall into as you go through daily life.

When you feel your dog pull; allow your hips and knee joints to soften, release and fill your lower back, and breathe into your entire rib cage. Now notice if it starts to reduce the force of the pull.

This concept also comes from the riding world, in the form of Connected Riding's "Neutral Pelvic". This neutral pelvis position is the only place that we as humans are biomechanically neutral, meaning that we are placing the least amount of stress on our joints and are best able to rebalance and move independently.

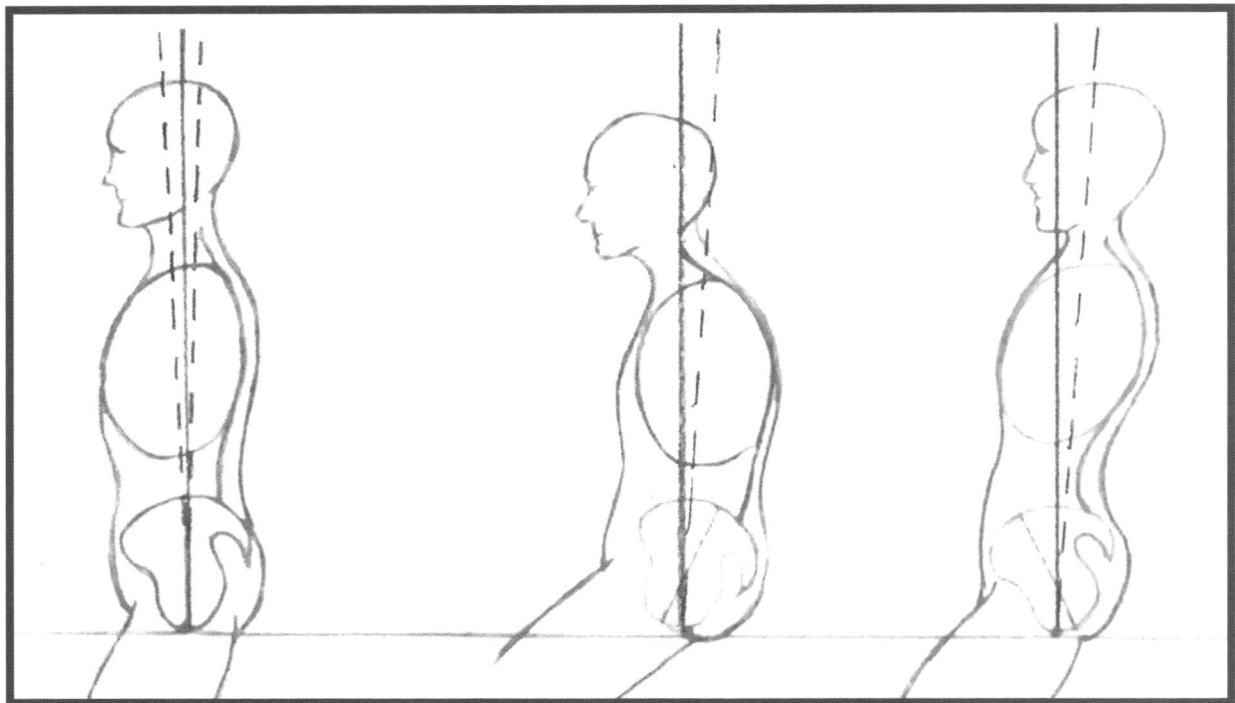

Peggy Cummings' Connected Riding recognizes 3 distinct postural tendencies, "Neutral", "Slumped" and "Arched". "Neutral" is the only posture that allows for free movement through the limbs and joints and puts the least amount of pressure and strain on the joints and soft tissue. When you find a "Neutral" posture you are better balanced and more solid without relying on more muscle strength or bracing.

Meet & Melt

Once you are no longer "water skiing" behind your dog, the next important change is in how you give your dog a signal, or communication, on the leash. The "takes one to know one" adage is very true when it comes to leash pulling in dogs. When most handlers experience a tug on the leash, their instant reaction, a reflex really, is to pull back. Thus begins the opposition reflex tug of war we have all experienced with a dog who pulls. If, instead of instantly pulling back, you were to meet the dog's pressure, pause, and then slowly melt (release your pressure) towards the dog's pulling pressure, you are often able to interrupt the dog's forward lean without completely throwing him out of balance.

This idea of "meeting and melting" to pressure comes from a Connected Riding concept for horses. Horses, like dogs, fall out of balance and will be on the forehand. Unlike dogs, horses weigh half a ton, literally, so there is no hope of a handler, or in this case a rider, being able to out muscle this with a corrective check – as is done with many dogs.

One component of helping a horse maintain balance will be how the rider uses the reins. Using a slow "ask and release", more subtly described as a "meet and melt" so it is done slowly, is generally one of the most effective ways to reduce how much weight the rider feels on the reins. Allow the motion to come through your softly bent elbow to avoid any locked joints. When the signal on the leash or reins is fluid and elastic, rather than a static pull, the dog, or horse, does not have anything to lean into and therefore will be encouraged to find their own balance.

Finding the Melt

Learning to "Meet and Melt" to pressure rather than instantly resisting it is definitely something that takes practice. It requires that you override basic instinct and do something that can seem very counter-intuitive. Practicing to "Meet & Melt" without a dog can be very useful.

A simple way to get the idea of this technique is to link your finger tips with your right thumb and left pinky finger closest to the ceiling and your left thumb and right pinky closest to the floor. Link your hands this way and center them on your midline, approximately level with your sternum.

Engage your right tricep muscles. Notice what happens to your left arm? It resists the pull and pulls back! Just like an out of balance dog and their handler! Now, think about slowly relaxing the muscles in your right tricep, without losing the link between your fingers. Notice that your left arm miraculously released its pull too!

Now practice this feeling of slowly releasing your pull by attaching a leash to a solid object, like a heavy table leg or railing. Allow yourself to pull, the inanimate object will certainly not start the opposition!

Once you get the hang of "melting" it can become a very positive habit anytime you feel pressure.

It takes a lot of conscious effort but it is possible to change you own default reaction from pull to melt. When you have achieved this you will be amazed at how much lighter and more effective your signals can be!

Stroke of Genius

The Tellington TTouch Method has long recognized that trying to "out pressure" an animal; that is matching whatever resistance they offering by applying an opposite pressure, and releasing only after the animal has; is not the most effective way of encouraging cooperation and softness. How we manage and reduce this "opposition response" has changed over the years. We initially used an "ask and release" motion when giving any signal on the leash, this is much more effective than a steady pressure but lacks finesse and can be abrupt.

Over the past few years there have been developments in refining and developing the subtlety and feel of this technique. Like many of the Tellington TTouch techniques, work with horses inspired refined techniques with dogs. After working with Peggy Cummings and incorporating Connected Riding tools, Sarah Fisher, TTouch UK Instructor, quickly realized that "Combing of the Leash" would have many beneficial applications for dogs.

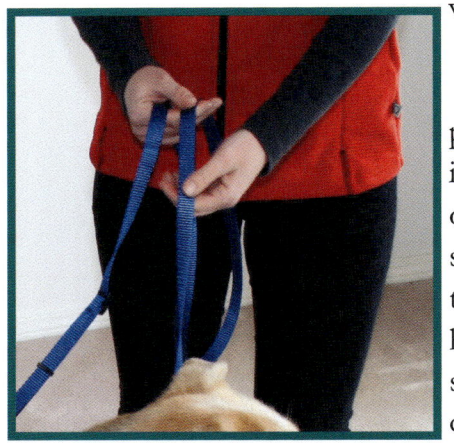

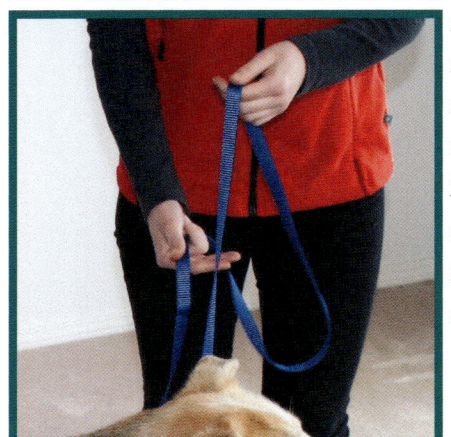

Teaching handlers to "Stroke the leash" (the technique as applied to dogs) is a simple and incredibly effective way of reducing the Opposition Response and changing the habitual patterns of the human. It also sends a different, non-habitual, type of signal to the dog that will likely get their attention. To "Stroke the leash" the handler simply slides their hands up the leash, hand under hand, (as though you were drawing a boat into shore), towards the navel, making a soft connection with the dog. This can be used in many instances whether it is to slow a rushing dog, make contact before giving a new signal, or redirecting a dog that is captivated by something in the opposite direction. You can also take this concept and train yourself to do a "micro slide" any time you feel pressure with the idea of interrupting a pulling movement from your dog. Training yourself to respond to pressure by allowing the leash to slide several millimeters, rather than having a 'death grip' on the leash, can often interrupt the Opposition Response before it starts.

The leash will be in two hands with one hand at the end of the leash . If the end of the leash is in the right hand, reach under the leash and pick up the leash between your thumb and forefinger, pause, and slide up the leash towards other hand. Repeat with the other hand. If you are working with a pulling dog you might find that starting with meeting your contact with an equal pressure to the dog's pull and then stroking – acts like a 'melt' ; then lighten the amount of pressure you are using. Talk to your dog ie: "let's go' or 'this way' as you look towards the path you want him to take. Be sure to keep the end of the leash in one hand to avoid having the end of the leash hang and swing.

Stroke Not Struggle

To make your Leash Stroking most effective, it is useful to practice it with another human at the other end of the leash. Stand across from your human "dog" with both of you holding the end of the leash. The "handler" can experiment with different pressures, the difference between having the end of the leash swinging as they stroke or having it in their hand, adding a "pause" between each pass of the hands, and finally how they use their body as a whole.

Being mindful of allowing your entire body to softly follow each hand left to right, in a slight rotation of the torso, will make a huge difference in how soft and fluid the motion will feel to the dog. You may also experiment with different pressures of stroking, adjusting it depending on how "pull-y" your "dog" is. Having a human to provide verbal feedback is incredibly useful when perfecting and refining any new skill.

The beauty of this technique is that it is incredibly simply to teach clients, can be used in virtually any situation, with any type of equipment, and that it REALLY works! Once you add Leash Stroking to your tool box you will wonder what you ever did without it.

Shrug it Off

Tellington TTouch Body Wraps are used extensively for dogs and horses to get a better sense of self-awareness in their body and improve confidence. People can also benefit from wearing Body Wraps as a way of changing postural habits that are creating tension, crookedness, or immobility. Body Wraps are not tight and do not inhibit movement in any way. The gentle pressure helps to activate the nervous system and reminds the body of tension patterns that have become so habitual that they feel "normal".

The "Shrug Wrap" is a great option if you tend to slouch or tighten through your shoulders or back. Either of these tendencies will greatly affect how well you communicate with your dog on leash. As an added bonus it is easy to put on your own.

Take a single elastic bandage and place it diagonally across your back. Take the long end and flip it over your shoulder, allowing the bandage to cross in the middle of your back. Bring the end back under your arm and fasten the ends together with Velcro, knot or safety pin.

Part 3 ~ Tools of the Trade

Step into any pet store and you cannot help but be overwhelmed by the myriad of equipment choices for walking a dog on leash. The tools vary from ineffective to down-right medieval and everything in between.

There is a lot of debate about whether certain types of equipment are harmful or and to what degree they do or do not cause discomfort or pain.

One of the most wonderful, and potentially difficult things about the Tellington TTouch Method is its ever-evolving nature. Every animal we work with provides us with invaluable lessons and often teaches us a new "tool" for our metaphoric tool box. This means that nothing is finite and we are always looking to improve the clarity, ease, and lightness in how we work with animals.

In our decades of working with thousands of dogs in every type of scenario we have found a well-fitted harness with two points of leash contact to be the most effective and humane means to walk a dog on leash. This set up helps maintain balance and control without using force or aversive pressure and discomfort.

Just the tip of the Iceberg!

The Tellington TTouch Method is a huge body of work that aims to address issues holistically.

There are countless techniques and exercises to address a plethora of issues, including leash skills, and common health and behaviour issues.

In this text we are only touching on some of the ways we help dogs by changing their balance through techniques and exercises on lead. Tellington TTouch Bodywork, TTouches, and other tools, such as specific Playground for Higher Learning obstacles, and TTouch Body Wraps complement our leash exercises and help integrate long term changes in behavior and posture.

Harnessing a Dog's Potential

When the Tellington TTouch Method first began working with dogs in the 1990s one of the first concepts carried over from horses was the connection between physical, mental and emotional balance. It was noted how many dogs seemed to be pulled out of balance when on one point of contact from the collar very similarly to how foals reacted when first being haltered. Collars did not provide the handler with many options when it came to influencing the animal's balance or directing their movement from their feet. Our solution with foals was to make a Figure 8 around their body out of rope to help guide and feel their body, for dogs, the solution was harnesses.

Many people will make the claim that it's not the equipment, it's how it's used, when defending any number of training tools. This is true, however, there are varying degrees as to what kind of harm any piece of equipment can inflict in the wrong hands. There is no doubt that head collars on dogs can be misused and cause neck damage, and some harnesses sit very low in front can cause shoulder injury. Having said that, neither head collars, nor harnesses are specifically designed to inflict pain as a way of influencing behavior. Conversely, no matter how they are used, choke chains, prong collars, and e-collars are designed to work, to some extent, because they cause discomfort and pain in the form of punishment.

Safety First

Unlike flat collars, Harnesses are not meant to be left on an unattended dog.

Dogs should only wear harnesses when they are working on lead or for short, supervised off leash time.

It is not uncommon for dogs to chew through harnesses if they are left on for extended periods of time, especially if they are not fit for the dogs comfort.

The combination of a well-fitted harness and two points of contact provides the handler with the possibility of enhancing a dog's balance rather than just correcting or distracting a behavior. This addresses the most common root cause of leash pulling, physical imbalance.

6 Reasons A Harness Will Stop Your Dog From Pulling

By Janet Finley TTouch Practitioner

As a TTouch practitioner I always want to choose equipment that will help the dog to succeed, so I start teaching loose lead walking by fitting a good harness – one that doesn't tighten on the dog and that has at least chest and back attachments – together with a double-ended lead.

This may seem counter-intuitive. After all, anyone who has seen a team of huskies, knows that dogs can pull pretty hard into a harness. But it is also the best tool I know to stop a dog pulling. Here are six reasons why.

1. It takes pressure off the neck.

A dog pulling into a collar around the neck pulls himself off balance and he therefore has to use you (pulling back against him) to balance himself. Pressure on the neck also restricts breathing, reducing the oxygen that reaches the brain, increasing anxiety and reactivity and reducing the ability to learn. Not to mention the risk of physical damage to the neck and spine and to the soft tissue in the throat from pulling hard into a collar. So the first thing we need to do if we want to teach a dog to walk on a loose lead is to get that pressure off his neck! A good harness means that we can take all pressure off the neck, connecting instead to the chest and/or back.

2. It allows two points of contact

When you attach the lead to one point on the dog, when the lead tightens, the dog's opposition reflex will mean that he pulls into it. This is the case whether the attachment is to the collar or the back of the harness, which is why attaching to the back of the harness only, encourages a dog to pull. When a dog has not yet learned to walk on a loose lead, the lead will tighten simply because his natural pace is faster than ours. But a good harness has at least two connection points, one on the chest and the other on the back, and we can connect to each of these with either end of a double-ended lead. Then, if one end of the lead tightens, we can meet that pressure and then release it, while taking up the other connection. Alternating between connections in this way means that there is nothing for the dog to pull against and the opposition reflex is not triggered.

3. It positions the dog naturally at your side

If you want your dog to walk on a loose lead, the ideal place for it to be is beside you, matching your pace and direction. Attaching a lead to a collar or the back of a harness, positions you firmly behind the dog – in the perfect position to encourage pulling! But when you add that front connection to the harness, with two points of connection, the dog moves naturally to be positioned with his shoulder at your side. This is a much more comfortable position to walk in and does not encourage pulling, which brings us to our next point.

4. It is more comfortable for your dog

Harnesses distribute any pressure across a much larger and less sensitive body area in the chest and flank, than the alternatives where pressure is concentrated in the neck or face. A well-fitted harness is therefore more comfortable for your dog than being led by a collar or wearing a head-collar. Combined with two points of connection, a fixed harness does not put unpleasant pressure on the dog, which makes the dog more relaxed and therefore less likely to pull. Note: harnesses that tighten on the dog work by creating an unpleasant sensation when the dog pulls, which is not comfortable and not recommended.

5. It gives you better influence and communication

Two points of contact on a harness give you much more influence on your dog's behaviour than a single point, and it increases your ability to communicate what you want to your dog. It can be helpful to think of the connection at the back as your "brake" and the front connection as your "steering". If you want your dog to slow down, a gentle lift upwards (rather than backwards) on the back connection, will slow your dog without unbalancing him or triggering the opposition reflex. Direction can be communicated very clearly using the connection at the front. This allows you to use the lead gently to reinforce your verbal communication, as a cue or a signal, rather than a correction.

6. It encourages your dog to walk in balance

Ultimately, to set your dog up to succeed in learning to walk on a loose lead, he first needs to learn to walk in his own balance, without leaning his weight against you through the lead. As we have seen, using a single point of contact on a collar works against this and encourages the dog to pull forward, putting the dog (and you!) out of balance. But using a harness with points of connection on the chest and back, encourages the dog to move his centre of gravity backwards so he is more balanced. And a dog that is physically balanced will also have better emotional balance and will therefore be better able to learn.

Decades ago, well-designed dog harnesses were few and far between. The first harnesses we used were the step-in harnesses in conjunction with either a head collar or a flat collar, so that we had two points of influence to help balance the dog.

Then the harness revolution really began. 'Sensation' harnesses came on the market and provided a good option. Its designer realized that the further forward the point of contact was on the dog, the less likely they were to pull, placing the leash ring attachment on the front of the chest. Unfortunately the harnesses did not have a top ring, which did not offer a second point of contact.

From the 'Sensation' a number of variations were developed – the 'Sensible'; 'Easy Walk' by Premier and the 'Halti' harness became the best known. While these can be effective, their fit around the dog's barrel and chest sits very low on the dog's shoulders (inhibiting some leg movement, which may be why it reduces pulling) and they generally pull forward into the elbows of the dog. Asymmetrical soreness, rubbing and gait irregularity has been reported in some dogs.

Today the most important criteria for any harness we use are; that it fits correctly, is comfortable for the dog and that there are suitable points for lead attachment. Harnesses that have rings too far back will often trigger pulling by creating a backward pressure to the leash.

Every harness has pluses and minuses – look for a harness that gives room for the dog's shoulders to move freely and has a front and back ring, ensuring that the ring on the dog's back is not too far back.

It is also important to consider your dog's individual needs when choosing a harness. Some short haired breeds may prefer a very soft material. Dogs who are head shy or sensitive about having their paws touched will prefer harnesses that can completely open to be put on (as opposed to having to put it over their heads, or lift their feet into the harness.

Today we are fortunate enough to have a market full of different harnesses so that dogs of all shapes and sizes can find one with an ideal fit and comfort.

Handling your dog with two points of contact help foster loose leash walking and a more relaxed, confident, demeanor.

Introducing A Harness

The majority of dogs are accepting of a harness so long as it fits well and is comfortable. For some dogs, anything unfamiliar is cause for concern so it is necessary to introduce a harness in small, low stress steps. If your dog seems concerned with the harness, either the sight of it or while it is being put on, chunk it down into steps and start with a Body Wrap *(see photo below). A simple Half or Quarter Wrap is often all that is needed to help a dog become comfortable with contact around their chest and barrel.

Let your dog move around with the Body Wrap on, making sure they do not go into freeze or fool around. If the dog does start to freeze, hold their breath, harden in the eye, grab at a leash or other object or keep rolling and offering their stomach, back off and chunk it down even more, leaving the wrap on only for short periods of time, even just laying it on the dog, untied. Encourage movement, do some TTouches and use treats if appropriate to positively reinforce the experience.

If your dog has been Clicker trained, you may incorporate targeting when introducing the harness.

Once your dog seems to find the Body Wrap acceptable, you may incorporate the harness. In some cases you can leave the Body Wrap on and add the harness over top. Like the Body Wrap, the Harness should only be left on for short periods of time initially. It is important for your dog to know that it will be taken off and that they do not have to resort to a very "loud" behavior to have it removed.

Wrapped Up

TTouch Body wraps are a simple yet incredibly effective tool that can help with a variety of behavioral and physical concerns.

A great way to use Body wraps is as a way to gently and mindfully introduce a dog to wearing a harness. All you need is a 2 or 3 inch cotton elastic bandage, preferably with Velcro closures.

Take the bandage, centered across the middle of the dog's chest and cross the ends over the top of the shoulders so that there is an "X" in the middle of the dog's shoulder blades.

For some dogs it is best to just let them feel the bandage undone and then take it off. If you dog does not seem overly concerned fasten the ends together so that the bandage is against the dog's body without being tight.

For more detailed information please refer to "All Wrapped Up: For Pets" by Robyn Hood & Mandy Pretty.

Be sure to keep the Harness relatively loose and adjusted so that it is not rubbing at the shoulder or elbow.

For dogs who are initially nervous about harnesses, be sure to choose a harness that does not need to be put over the head or stepped into. As with the Body Wrap, encourage movement and use TTouches and treats as appropriate.

Harness shy?

Some people report that their dogs "don't like the harness" when first switching from a collar to a harness. Most dogs wear collars all the time and become habituated to them. Sometimes what seems like aversion is simply that the harness feels unfamiliar.

If your dog seems to react negatively to seeing a harness, even after a few uses, you have several options.

First: Check the fit. Sometimes an ill-fitting harness can be causing discomfort. Check that the sternum piece is long enough that the harness is not rubbing into the elbow or that the chest piece is not so low that it is pulling across the point of the shoulder.

Second: Depending on the type of skin or coat, or level of overall sensitivity, some dogs are very sensitive to the type of material a harness is made out of. Fleece harnesses or fleece sleeves that cover existing material can be a good option.

Third : Some dogs are quietly, or not so quietly, concerned about things going over their head and therefore have a negative association with the harness, depending on the brand. What can you do? Go backwards and chunk it down into smaller pieces. Start with a few TTouches ("Getting in TTouch with Your Dog" L Tellington Jones) all around the dog's body, add a Body Wrap ("All Wrapped Up: For Pets", R.Hood); and then a Rope Harness (See Equipment Hack chapter) – these exercises change how a dog feels in their own body and breaks down the experience of wearing a harness into small, low stress steps.

Fourth: Try a different harness! No style of harness works for every dog or situation.

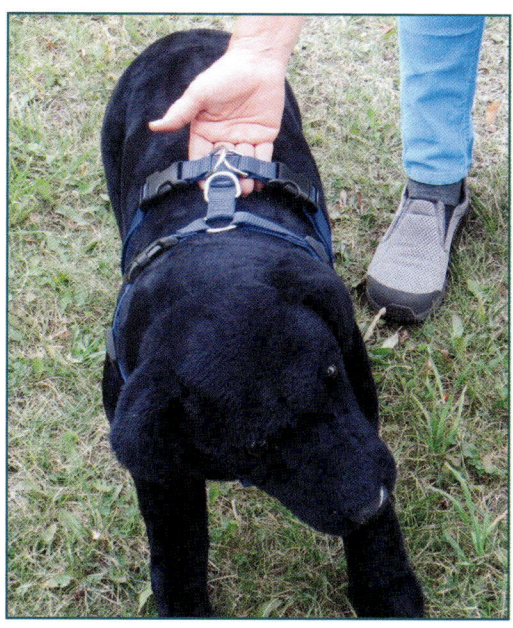

Fitting the Harness

Correctly fitting any Harness is extremely important. While each make and model will have specific fit characteristics and instructions, there are several areas to note when fitting any harness.

Always open all of the harness's clips that you can. This may seem obvious but many well-designed harnesses open so it does not have to be put over the dog's head. When you are working with an "easy going" dog, especially one you know well, it is tempting to keep the head piece attached so that you just slide it over the dog's head, instead of undoing it and snapping it around the neck. While this may be totally fine, some dogs will eventually become head shy from sliding the harness over their head and ears.

Any harness should lay flat against the dog's body. If you are using a harness that has a connector strap between the front legs you will want to check that this strap is flush against the sternum but not so short that it is pulling the barrel strap into the elbows.

When checking for fit, be sure and notice how tight or loose it is when your dog is standing, sitting, and lying down. Your dog's movement should not be inhibited at all, and it is worth paying special attention to how the harness fits in relation to your dog's shoulders and elbows.

After removing a harness, it is a good idea to reattach all of the clips so it does not become tangled in storage.

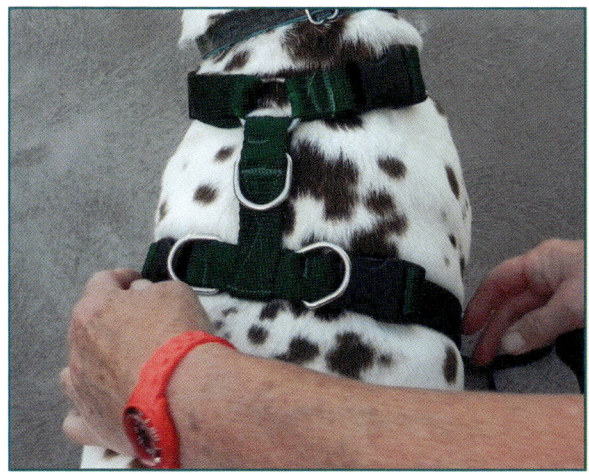

This harness has been fitted too tightly and will be very uncomfortable for the dog to move or sit in. The handler is unable to slide their fingers between the dog and the harness.

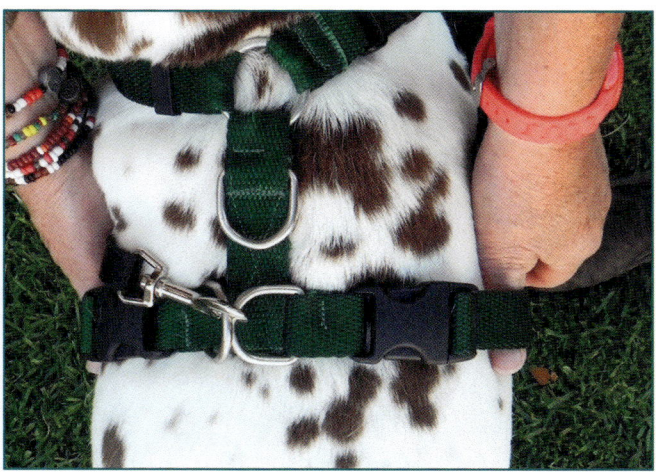

Here the harness has been properly adjusted. There is just enough room for a hand to slide under the harness.

Leashes:
The Long & the Short Of It

While seemingly simple and unremarkable, leashes can have a huge impact in how easily a dog can walk in balance. In addition to harnesses we also find that some leash designs will foster more appropriate leash walking habits. Double ended leashes and leashes with sliding handles are two pieces of equipment that are invaluable.

Ideally leashes, for this type of exercise, are not longer than 6 to 8 feet long. As the law of 'equal and opposite' dictates, the farther back the handler gets, the farther forward the dog will get. Of course this does not mean that long training leashes are not invaluable for safely teaching dogs recall before going off leash or for just allowing your dog to roam and sniff. They are not particularly useful for teaching a dog to walk in balance near the handler.

The weight of a leash should also be taken into consideration. Obviously hardware must be strong enough not to break from a safety standpoint, especially with large, pulley dogs. However, very heavy hardware and leash material, especially on smaller dogs can affect balance and symmetry and negative long term effects. Ideally the leash material, hardware and snaps should be as small and light as possible, while still being strong enough to contain the dog in a "worst case" scenario.

Retractable Leashes?

The dangers of retractable leashes have recently become mainstream information with reports of rope burn and deep abrasions caused by the narrow retractable cord getting caught around limbs or fingers of dogs and/or handlers.

Dangers aside, retractable leashes also apply non-stop pressure to the dog which triggers more pull and puts them into a habit of pressing against the leash, even though it is not "hard" pressure.

While retractable leashes are no doubt convenient, users must be extremely careful with their use.

They should not be used in conjunction with no-pull harnesses or head collars and only with dogs who are very reliable on leash. Since they do not provide the handlers with a clear form of communication and can easily tangle and inadvertently create a constant pull signal unbeknownst to the handler.

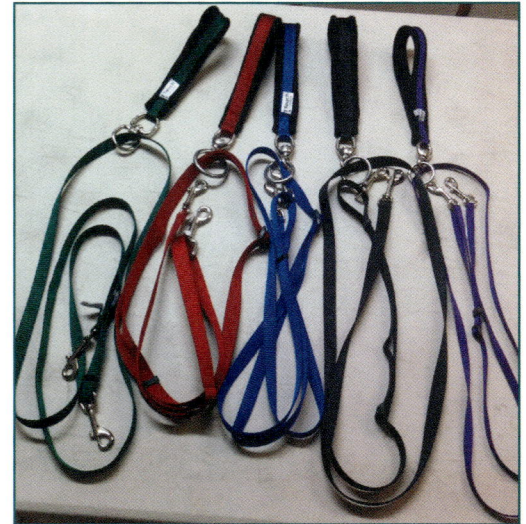

Whatever leash you choose should be comfortable for yourself and your dog and support the principles of a balanced, relaxed posture. We find that a 6 to 8 foot, double ended leash is the most effective leash for helping encourage balance and confidence in dog and handler. The exception may be with a tall person & small dog or small person and tall dog.

The TTouch Harmony Leash and handle set feature an adjustable length leash, sliding handle and double ended leash, perfect for Two Points of contact and loose leash walking.

Two are better than One: Two Points of Contact

A critical element to re-educating a dog and handler about walking on the leash is achieving and maintaining balance. One of the most effective ways to do this is by leading a dog with Two Points of Contact.

Tellington TTouch has been using the concept of leading with Two Points of Contact since the early 1990s. Today, many companies manufacture double ended leashes and harnesses with front and back hardware.

As explained in earlier chapters, leading a dog with Two Points of Contact provides the handler with influence over the dog's feet and body which is not possible with a single point of contact. A leash with a light snap on either end is ideal for leading with two points of contact. Placing one end on a ring at the chest and the other as far forward on the back as possible will give the handler the optimal position to rebalance and support a dog who tends to pull on the leash.

With Two Points of Contact the handler can use each end independently so that they can help to shift the dog's weight up and back towards the hind quarters without tightening the dog through the neck, back and shoulders.

Unlike only one point of contact, control or influence is not dependent on pulling back or turning the dog towards you. With a chest and back attachment, the handler can help contain the dog's movement without sacrificing balance or putting the dog into an awkward, potentially detrimental long term, posture.

As with any leading technique, using a "Meet and Melt" (pg 9) or "Stroke and Stride" (30)signals are the most effective in positively affecting a dog's balance.

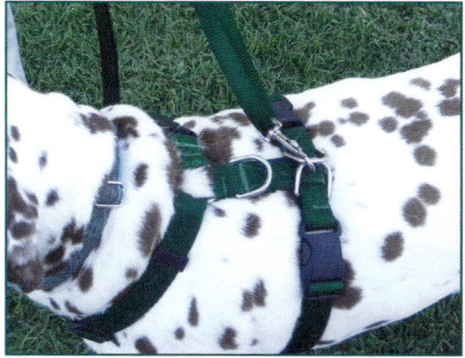

To use Two Points of Contact your harness should have a chest ring and a back ring that's not set too far behind the shoulders.

Can You Handle It?

One of the draw backs to using Two Points of Contact is that it is somewhat dependent on the mindfulness of the handler. As effective as this technique is, we found that it is not always embraced by owners and it is nearly impossible to implement when walking more than one dog, carrying a bag or pushing a carriage.

The introduction of the "Freedom Harness Leash" and now the TTouch Harmony Leash and Handle provide a great alternative, leash handles.

These specialty leashes are double ended with an independent, sliding handle on a ring, with a swivel in the case of the TTouch Harmony Leash and Handle. The sliding nature of the handle means that there is no fixed point of contact to trigger opposition and gives the handler a fluid, elastic contact without needing any particular technique to be successful.

The double ended leash and handle configuration can make Loose Leash walking easy for practically any dog/handler combination.

Leash Handles help reduce the Opposition Response triggered by a handler inadvertently pulling, tightening or grabbing the leash. In effect, the Leash Handles create a similar feeling as Leash Stroking or Meet and Melt might, without requiring as much conscious effect on the part of the handler.

The effectiveness of these handles is impressive and as with all new ideas, we began experimenting with new possibilities and applications. Adding just the handle to any leash with Two Points of Contact is incredibly effective and makes huge changes in how easily most dogs can walk on a loose leash.

Walking in balance with a handle is much easier to teach than Two Points of Contact and gives the dogs very clear, effective signals to stop, go, and turn.

Tellington TTouch Harmony Leash & Swivel Handle

Inspired by the Freedom Leash sliding handle, Robyn Hood developed the Harmony Leash and Handle as a complement to the TTouch Harmony Harness.

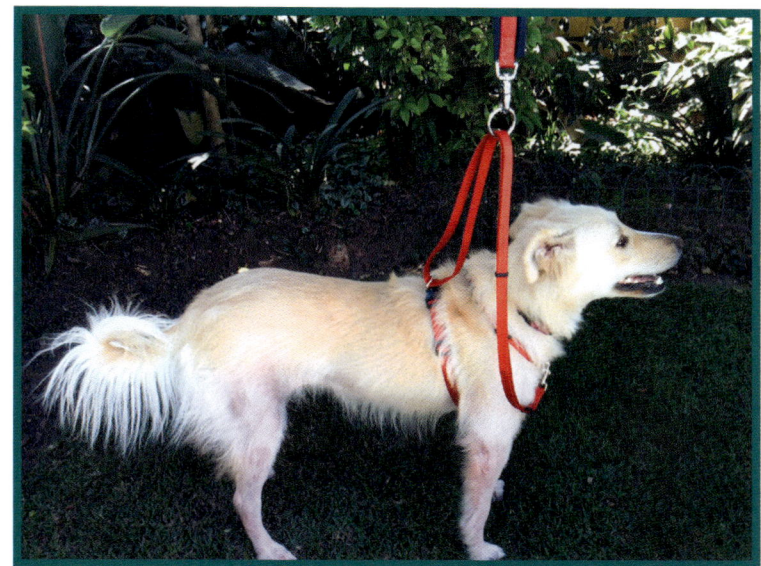

The leash itself is adjustable in length and allows for versatility and ease of use for the handler and the handle has a swivel which is less likely to tangle or twist the leash.

All snaps and hardware on the leash are lightweight yet durable so as not to interfere with the dog's balance or comfort.

Both the adjustable Harmony Leash and Harmony Handle can be used together, for optimal results, or on their own. The TTouch Harmony Harness is designed with this leash/handle set in mind.

This addition to the Tellington TTouch Method has made the quest for loose leash walking even easier to attain by helping the dog and handler find a balanced connection.

TTouch Harmony Leash Handles can be added to virtually any smooth, double ended leash to help encourage loose leash walking and a calm, confident walking partner.

Part 4 ~ Leading in Balance

One of the core components of the Tellington TTouch Method are leading and groundwork exercises. Each technique has the same goals; teaching dogs how to find balance and be in harmony with their human counter parts. Finding overall balance is one of the most important pieces in the quest for relaxed, cooperative, Loose Leash walking.

Dogs who are in better balance physically, tend to be so emotionally as well. It is very common to see a reduction in on-leash dog reactivity as physical balance improves.

Helping dogs find balance, and self-carriage leads to an increased feeling of safety, which fosters self-confidence. When dogs feel safe and confident they are better able to act rather than react, and make better choices in their everyday lives. Each of the following exercises can be used to change the way a dog feels in his body and is able to find his balance.

When dogs are balanced they tend not to pull on the leash and are generally less anxious and reactive to outside stimuli.

Depending on what you have available to you, in terms of equipment, the Tellington TTouch Method offers several ways to help dogs find balance on leash, without using pressure or punishment. The Balance Leash, Double Ended Leash, and TTouch Harmony Leash and Handle each offer ways to help dogs find self-carriage and balance, reducing leash pulling and on-leash reactivity.

Longer leash?

While a leash that is too can create issues if your dog is unbalanced, a leash that is too short can limit the enjoyment your dog has while on walks. A longer leash will let your dog enjoy the benefits of sniffing. When you want him to come with you, keep the leash loose and try to use your voice to ask him to come rather than automatically giving a leash signal.

For dogs, having the chance to sniff along their walks is a lot like us reading our daily newspaper...or newsfeed if we're being more current! Remember that walks are not just about exercise, they are also about mental stimulation and a time when you can build your relationship with your dog.

Balance Leash Techniques

The Balance Leash is one of the original Tellington TTouch leading tools for dogs. It is one of the simplest and easy to use techniques, and has the versatility to be used on the fly with virtually any type of leash or harness/collar configuration. This makes the Balance Leash a fantastic tool for shelter workers or for any situation when you are unable to use a harness and two points of contact. It can come in handy if your dog regularly walks on a loose leash but occasionally needs help coming back into balance. If your dog regularly needs help walking in balance, it is advised to use one of the other options such as a harness and sliding handle.

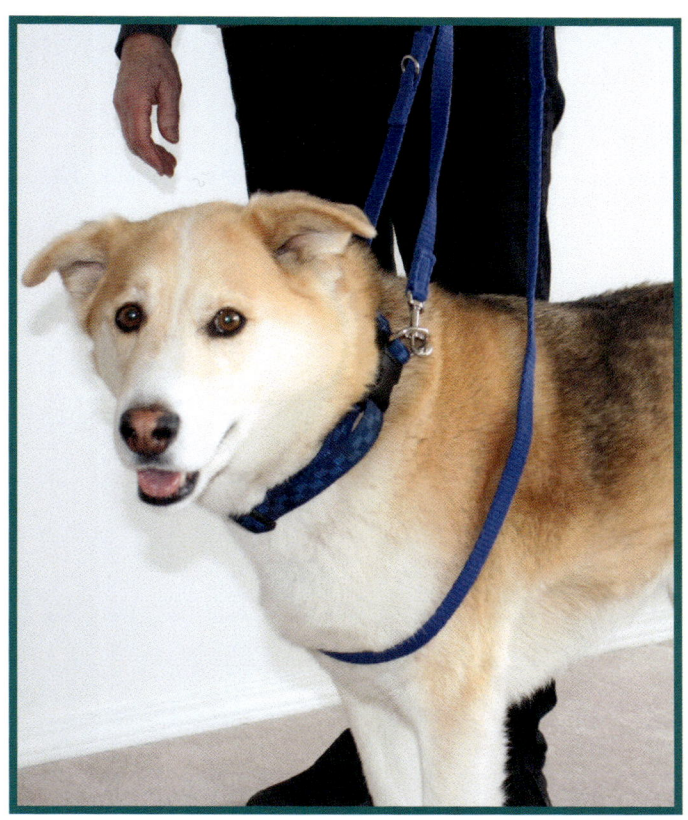

Balance Leash

It is simple and a very effective means to stop pulling and help bring a dog into balance. It is a great way to take pressure off of the neck and rebalance a pulling or reactive dog when you do not have any extra tools available.

You can use nearly any 6'-8' leash (depending on the height of the person and the dog) with this technique to influence a dog's balance Stop the dog and maintain contact on the collar to prevent the dog from moving forward while you move up the leash, gathering a loop or two in your hand, so you are standing near the dog's collar. Transfer the leash into the hand furthest away from the dog.

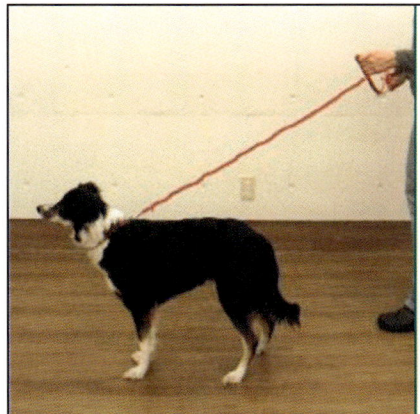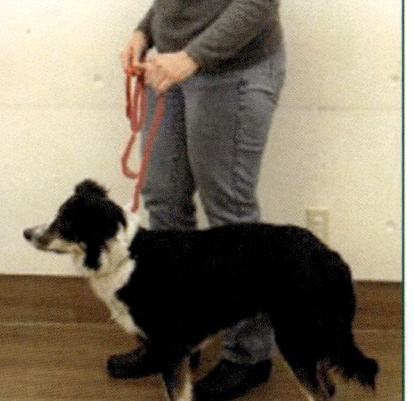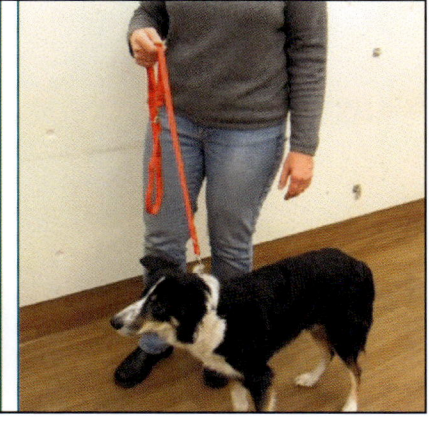

Put the back of your hand nearest the dog on the side of your thigh. Bring your hand under the leash and grasp it. As you turn your hand you will see that this directs the remainder of the leash toward the opposite side of the dog.

Take the hand with the remainder of the leash and drop the loop(s) on the opposite side of the dog from where you are standing. This hand will now just be holding the end of the leash.

Exhale while you bring the leash across the front of the dog. Remember to stand in balance, not leaning or reaching forward. Position the leash across the middle of the dog's chest. Adjust the location of the hand near the collar to take the pressure off the collar yet close enough to allow you to pick up the connection if you want to use it to ask the dog to move.

Your hips will be turned slightly toward the dog in order to be in a comfortable, balanced position.

If the leash is very long, you may need to pick up a loop with your outside hand in order to rebalance the dog and remain in position near the collar.

If your dog pulls use a "Meet & Melt" (pg 15) signal with the line across the chest in a slightly upward fashion. Take care not to draw the lead upward onto the throat. Ideally the signal is across the sternum and top of the point of the shoulder (think of gently lifting horse reins with both hands.

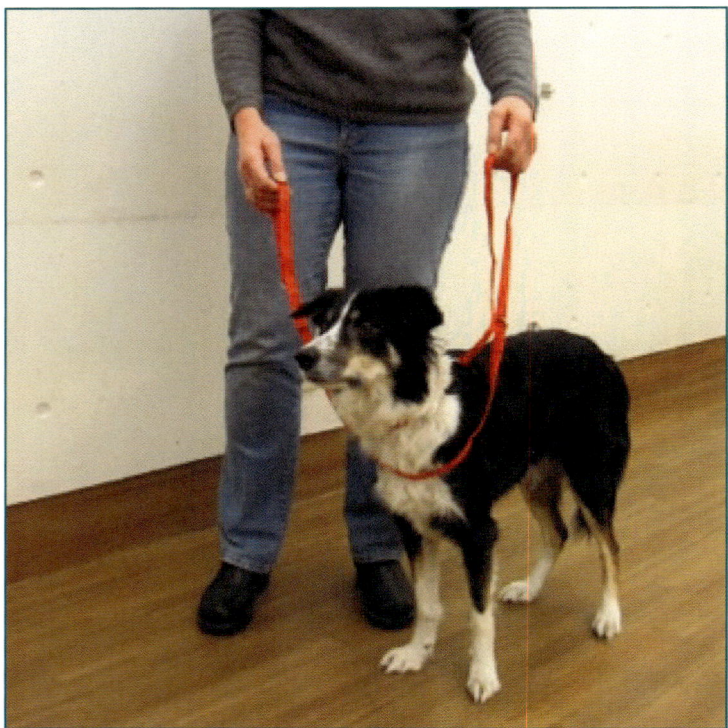

The Balance Leash, ready to help take pressure off of the collar.

The Balance Leash is especially effective on medium to large sized dogs.

If your dog pulls occasionally, in especially arousing situations for example, the Balance Leash may be an ideal tool to use in a pinch to help your dog relax and come back into balance. Once you are practiced with this technique you can bridge the leash and use with one hand.

In a Pinch?

While not ideal for everyday pullers or dogs who tend to fall out of balance habitually, the Balance Leash and Balance Leash Plus are fantastic tools to use in situations where you do not have access to well fitted harnesses. In the veterinary office it keeps dogs from pulling towards other dogs; for vet techs and groomers when moving dogs in the office; in dog training class while waiting or when walking to and from class to keep practicing walking in balance. Or in shelter situations where dogs may be stressed and pulling on the leash. Not only helpful for dogs but may help prevent back stress for handlers.

The Balance Leash configurations give you the ability to take pressure off of the neck and help the dog find their feet which helps them feel safer and less anxious.

Balance Leash Plus

This variation on the Balance Leash was developed for smaller dogs or for those dogs that back out of the Balance Leash. The Balance Leash Plus creates the same re-balancing signal as the Balance Leash, but has added stability.

Standing as you would for the regular Balance Leash, take the leash behind your dog's opposite elbow and up in between the front legs. You can either use it like this or bring the end of the leash up through the dog's collar at the front which helps "lock" the leash into place so it does not slide laterally. This also helps keep the leash from slipping up or the dog from turning out of it, especially with smaller animals.

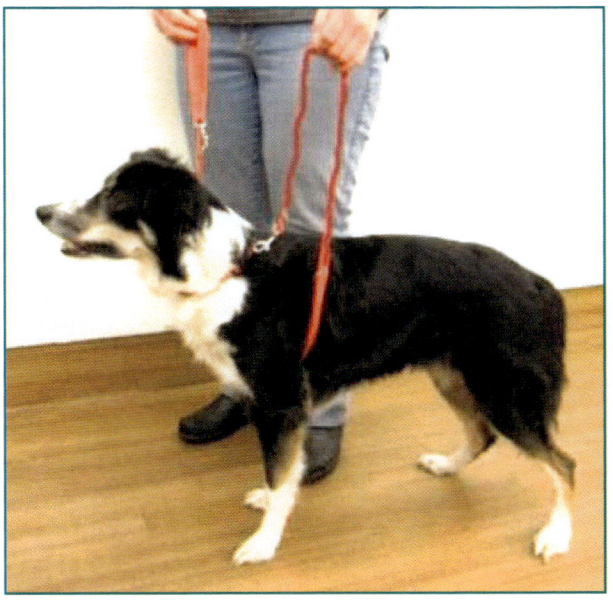
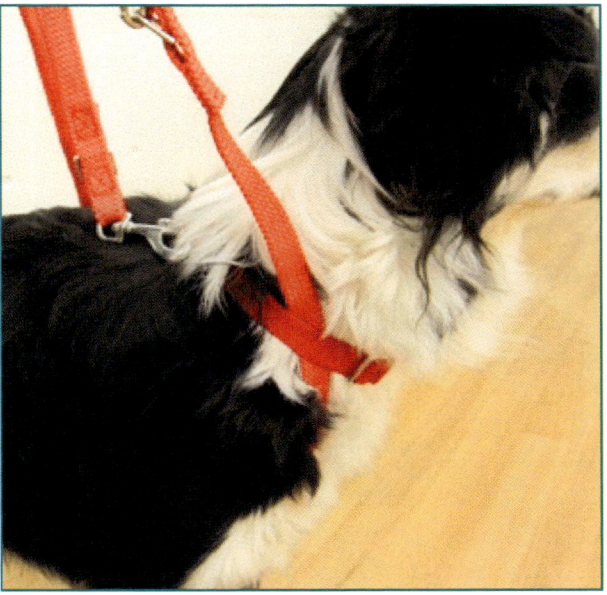

As with the Balance Leash it is most effective if you stay at the dog's shoulder and use an upward "Meet & Melt" signal on the leash.

Double Ended Leash

As we have established, 'Two Points of Contact' is one of the most useful ways to help a dog come into balance while walking on the lead. The Balance Leash techniques are wonderful tools to create Two Points of Contact when you only have a regular, flat leash. For regular use it is ideal to have a flat, double ended leash. One end snapped to the chest ring of the harness, the other to the back ring on top. This provides an opportunity to rebalance a pulling dog and reduces the amount of opposition that a handler may inadvertently place on the lead.

Walking with a Double Ended Leash is most effective if you hold the leash in two hands, with the leash being held between your thumb and forefinger. Holding the leash like a "driving rein" will lesson any reflexive, gross motor control and encourage fine motor control. Once your dog is walking on a loose leash there is no reason not to hold the leash in one hand.

If you have a very strong dog and are a small person or have arthritic hands you might find holding the leash around your baby fingers is easier for you – just be aware of doing your best to avoid constant backward pull.

In most situations holding the leash in a "driving rein" way , so that your thumb is at the dog end of the leash, is ideal and does not trigger "gross-motor" control.

For handlers who suffer from arthritis or if you are handling an exceptionally large dog you may choose to hold the leash with your baby fingers nearest the dog.

Making a Graceful Exit

There are times when you just have to move a dog out of a situation. In most cases people just use their arms and pull This is often unsuccessful or escalates the situation. The problem is that as we pull, our arms straighten, putting both the human and the dog out of balance, triggering Opposition, making cooperation less likely.

To make a 'Graceful Exit'', meet the dog's pressure and take a step towards the dog so you can bend your elbows which puts you in better balance over your feet. This allows the dog to come back into balance over his feet. Move your feet and step calmly backward, rotate and move in another direction. It is so important to move your body as a unit; stay balanced over your feet and avoid the pulling with your arms. Once a dog is over their feet they 'can' move with you.

This can really only be done with a harness, otherwise you are pulling on the dog's neck.

The "Graceful Exit" is a great exercise to practice with a friend so you can feel how it works.

The person playing the "dog" begins to lean. The handler usually meets this lean with a pull - it is reflex. Handler should take a step towards the dog allowing a bend in their elbow.

As the handler stands in balance they pause and start to walk backwards, maintaining bent elbows and soft joints.

The "dog" is able to come into balance and move with the handler without pulling.

The key is to keep your elbows next to your body and move your feet.

If your dog is particularly habituated to forging ahead, is habitually out of balance, or is in a very reactive in certain situations, there are several techniques that can be used to help rebalance and refocus your dog to interrupt the Opposition Response when using a Double Ended Leash.

Technique #1 "Meet & Melt"

"Meet & Melt" is one of the number of techniques to have on hand ANY time you feel a pull or the hint of resistance when handling an animal in any situation, regardless of what type of equipment you are using.

How to do it

As described on page 9, to diffuse a pull with "Meet & Melt", simply "Meet" the pressure of the pull, pause, and slowly "Melt" to release the pressure, incrementally so that you do not "drop" the dog. If you are holding the leash in two hands you can either think about "Meet and Melt" with both hands simultaneously or alternately. Regardless of which you use, be sure that you "Meet" in an upward motion rather than back. A slow "Melt" rather than a quick release allows the dog to come back into balance rather than falling into the lean.

Technique #2 "Quarter Turn"

Using a "Quarter Turn" to help re-balance and slow a pulling dog works in two ways. One, it rebalanced your dog off of the forehand and two it helps put the handler into a more forward position, reducing any inadvertent backward pressure.

How to do it

As you want to slow and stop, think about walking your feet as you quarter turn your body towards the dog, giving an upward signal on the chest, melting and exhaling and you walk into a halt. If your dog is slightly out of balance you may have to repeat the quarter turn and upward signal.

A "Quarter Turn" puts the handler in a more effective position to rebalance the dog.

Technique #3 "Stroke & Stride"

The "Stroke & Stride" is a great technique to use if your find yourself getting too far behind a dog that is pulling.

How to do it

Stroke the leash attached to the front of the harness, hand under hand, as you keep moving forward towards the dog's head, moving along side of the dog. Stroke in an up direction rather than back to help makes it is easier for the dog to stop in balance.

Using the TTouch Harmony Leash & Handle

The various Balance Leash and Double Ended Leash configurations were a go-to mainstay in the TTouch toolbox for years and are still used in situations where the only available equipment is a standard leash. As effective as these techniques are, the drawback is that they require two hands, making it potentially awkward for handlers especially when walking more than one dog at a time.

A wonderful, user friendly and effective solution is the Harmony Leash Handle. This configuration is ideal for everyday walking and handling or when working to help change an extreme puller. It takes little effort on the handler's part and helps dogs find their balance without force.

Handling Yourself

Experiencing what certain leash signals feel like is a great way to gain new insights about what might be effective and clear for your dog. Putting yourself on the other end of the leash and handle is a great way to hone your technique and experience what works and what does not.

With a friend, take a double ended leash with a handle.   Whoever is going to be the "dog" first takes the front /chest snap in their hand closest to the handler. The back snap is held at the crook of the elbow, anchored by the outside hand. The "dog" should remember to keep their nose pointed in the same direction as their hands.

This exercise allows people to feel how the sliding feeling of the handle reduces the reflex to pull and gives you insight as to how you can really fine tune exercises and signals by putting yourself in the "Dog's Paws".

Trade off who is the dog and who is the handler and experiment with being "pull-y", "lag-y" or "distracted" so the handler can practice their skills too!

If you think it is the same as using two hands on the leash - try the same exercise without the handle and two hands on the leash and notice the difference.

The Harmony Leash Handle is a simple tool that can be added to virtually any flat Double Ended Leash. The handle is on a swivel ring, slides along the leash, reduces resistance and prevents the handler from inadvertently creating an oppositional pull. The Harmony Leash Handle was inspired by the Freedom No-Pull Harness double connection leash and handle set. Handles helps reduce pulling but they are on a fixed ring and can become tangled and twisted if the dog turns in circles.

As the swivel Harmony Handle slides it moves with the dog while maintaining a dynamic connection. As you ask the dog to turn the signal shifts between the front harness ring attachment and the back ring which helps reduce opposition helping your dog stay more balanced. When used in conjunction with the adjustable Harmony Leash, it is an incredibly versatile and effective piece of equipment that gently allows for balanced, relaxed, loose leash walking.

The Harmony Leash is an adjustable length leash with lightweight, yet durable, double snap ends. This allows for chest and back attachment to help encourage a more balanced posture for dog and handler. Attach the smaller of the two clips, if there are two sizes, to the front ring on the chest and the larger snap to the rings or ring furthest back on the harness.

Using this configuration of Handle and Leash is quite effortless and with a few simple techniques you can easily troubleshoot some of the most habitual leash pullers.

Handle Hints

It is important to use any piece of equipment safely. When using the Harmony Leash Handle be sure to keep the fleece loop held in your palm.

Avoid putting your hand through the loop. This could cause injury to your wrist should your dog, especially a large one, pull suddenly.

Turning with a Leash Handle

Moving your dog with a sliding point of connection can seem challenging at first, in reality it is simply good use of body language to guide your dog in the direction you would like to go. Depending on the length of your leash you can make a turn away from you, towards the dog, by just taking your hand across the dog's back, allowing the handle to slide.

If this signal is not clear enough for your dog, try holding the handle in your outside hand and slide the back of your other hand under the leash and over the dog's back; thus moving the leash towards the dog. Keep thinking forward with your outside hand and move your feet in the direction you would like to go.

Turning Harley to the right, Robyn simply takes the handle in the direction in which she would like him to move. This is a bit like 'neck reining' a horse and is sometimes easier with a shorter leash.

If your leash is too long you may have to take the handle in the hand furthest from the dog and use the back of your hand to slide the leash over the dog's back to indicate the turn.

Steps to Loose Leash Walking

For many dogs, simply incorporating the leash and handle will help foster easy, loose leash walking habits. If your dog has a very ingrained habit of pulling or you and your dog are in a distracting situation, you may need to incorporate some easy techniques to help your dog find balance and allow for a loose leash.

Since there is no 'one size fits all' solution for every dog and every situation it is important to keep all of your options in mind when confronted with leash pulling. Try a technique and notice the response. If one technique doesn't work, try another!

Having options allows us as handlers to be flexible and meet the needs of the immediate situation. Having the freedom to change what we're doing makes for a more successful and positive outcome in the long and short term.

Technique #1 The Post

A common way to work with a pulling dog is to stop and be like a neutral 'post', then wait for your dog to release the pull or come back to you. This reduces your contribution to the "pulling match", creating a neutral point of contact.

How to Do it

As soon as you feel pressure on the leash, simply place both hands through the handle and bend your elbows to keep your hands close to your body and stop your feet. This prevents the handler from adding to the pull dynamic.

Once you have mastered "Meet and Melt"(pg 15) add it to your "Post" to reduce pulling even more quickly.

As the dog comes into balance and lightens on the leash, turn your body, call the dog enthusiastically and walk in the other direction - without pulling on the lead.

Troubleshooting

If "The Post" is not working, ensure that you are not inadvertently pulling with your arms. To be most effective your arms should be passively resting next to your body, with your elbows bent.

It is also important to keep your body in a neutral posture, aligning your ear, shoulder, hip and ankle bone. Many people will habitually lean back and tighten their lumbar area when standing, this makes any contact on the leash feel stronger than you realize.

Technique #2 Meet & Melt

As discussed earlier, "Meet & Melt" is one of the number one techniques to have on hand ANY time you feel a pull or the hint of resistance when handling an animal in any situation, regardless of what type of equipment you are using. Developed by Peggy Cummings "Connected Riding" method, "Meet & Melt" trains the handler to diffuse the "Opposition Reflex" without throwing the animal out of balance.

How to Do it

As soon as there is pressure on the leash, most dogs will go into "Opposition" and lean—putting them out of balance. To diffuse pulling by using "Meet & Melt", simply "Meet" the pressure of the pull, pause, and slowly "melt" to release the pressure, incrementally so that you do not "drop" the dog. A slow "Melt" rather than a quick release allows the dog to come back into balance rather than falling into the lean.

Sally has spotted a new dog coming down the yard , causing her to pulls forward on the leash. With bent elbows and both hands in the handle, Robyn meets her forward pull and maintains a neutral posture.

Robyn slowly releases the pressure on the leash and you can see that even though she is still aroused by the dog, the leash has slack and she is showing self-control and not taking a step.

Troubleshooting

If your dog is not responding to "Meet & Melt" try making the "Melt" slower. An abrupt release will just put the dog more out of balance and send them forward.

 Notice if you are holding your breath or have locked any joints in your body. Mindful breathing and soft joints make "Meet & Melt" much more effective.

Technique #3 Turn & Walk

The "Turn & Walk" technique is a great way to "reset" your position since it automatically puts the handler ahead and gets you out of the "Water Skier" position.

How to do it

As your dog pulls forward, step forward, towards his inside shoulder as you take your inside hand forward in front of you and your dog and gently rotate your body away from your dog while stepping ahead.

Look in the direction that you want to go and keep your feet moving with the leash is loose and relaxed. The handle will slide forward on the leash.

If you feel pressure on the leash as you are turning - allow your body—extend your arm & step **into** the direction of the dog, and the leash, to move in the direction that you feel the pressure, think "Meet and Melt", even though this will feel completely counter intuitive.

In the moment of release, the dog is able to come back into balance without the pressure of the leash putting them into an Opposition Response.

As you feel the tension or pull diminish, simply keep moving in the direction you want to go and engage your dog with your voice..

Robyn is asking Sally to leave her "person" and her dog friend. Robyn uses her body language, voice, and position to ask Sally to come along. By not pulling Sally does not go into "Opposition" and is able to comply.

Troubleshooting

If Turn & Walk does not seem effective, check that you are keeping your feet in motion and are not accidentally pulling on the leash. Remember that we also have a strong instinctive response to pull back to pressure.

You may also have to mindfully "pause" after you have tried to "Meet & Melt" on the leash so the dog has a chance to get back into balance.

As you turn, it is very helpful to verbally engage the dog without any pressure on the leash.

Technique #4 The Wheel

The "Wheel" technique helps the handler momentarily "pause" and rebalance the dog so that a better more "neutral" position can be attained.

How to do it

To offset pulling with the "Wheel", maintain the same pressure on the lead as you take your hand up and forward so it is directly above where the leash attaches to the harness. You should **not** feel as though you lift the dog. The leash should just have enough pressure so that you feel contact. Once you feel this slowly "Melt" the contact .

When the signal on the leash is up rather than back, it allows the dog's weight to shift so that the dog can come back over their feet into balance.

You can also use the "Wheel" while moving your feet forward - maintain the pressure you feel but take the leash up and forward then "Melt" the contact down as you keep your feet moving.

Troubleshooting

Make sure the leash is short enough so you don't have to lift your hand too high, or use the Ttouch Connector.

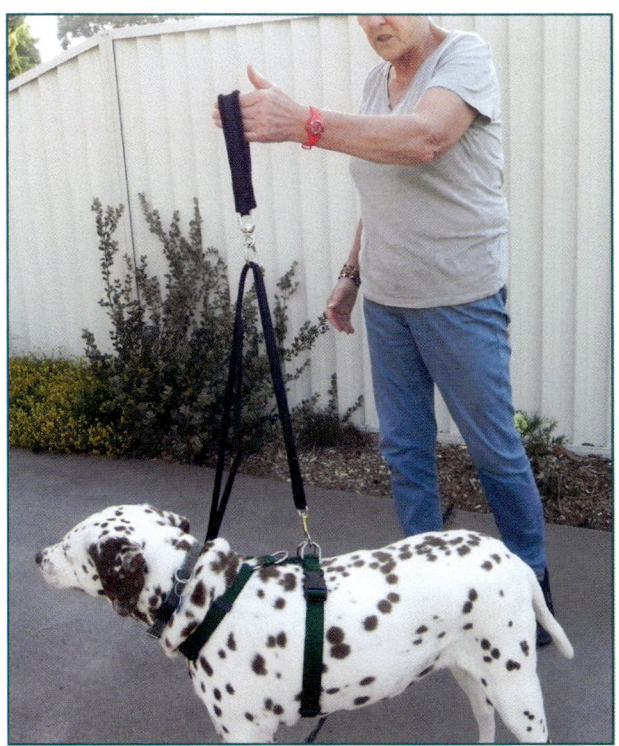
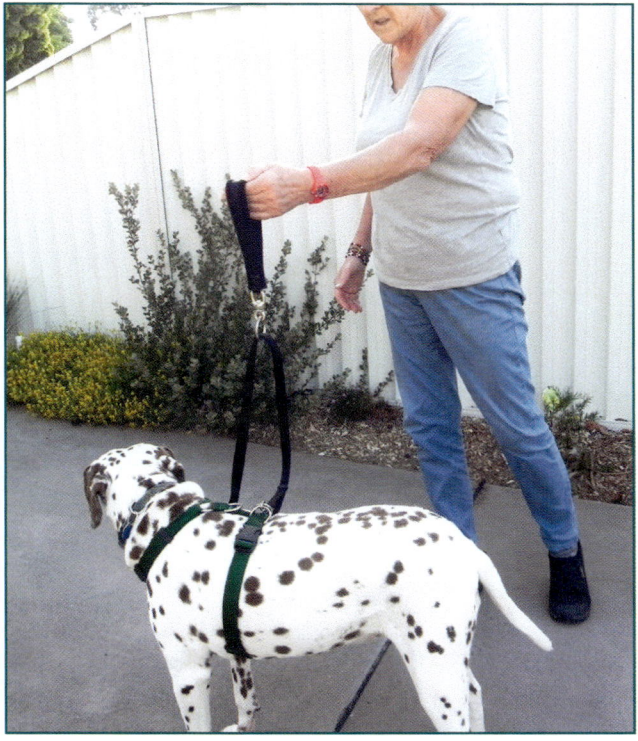

Case Study: "The Wheel" & Sally the Lab

Sally came to a training with Robyn in South Africa. Upon arrival she was described as "never moving slowly", on leash or off. She perpetually pulled on leash and was habitually out of balance.

Robyn used a TTouch Harmony Harness and Leash Handle Set to work with Sally. The change was immediate, Sally was able to walk slowly and calmly. The addition of "Meet & Melt" and "The Wheel" helped her find even better balance and relaxation.

Handler is behind dog - opposition back to front; keeping same amount of contact handler steps forward taking the handle up as she steps forward.– this moves the 'opposition' from back to front, to up and down, allowing dog to shift weight back into balance. Handler can now slowly melt the contact, so the leash is loose, and steps forward.

Leash is loose and handler's hand is over the shoulder, keep feet moving forward and allow dog to have the experience of a loose leash.

TTouch Connector

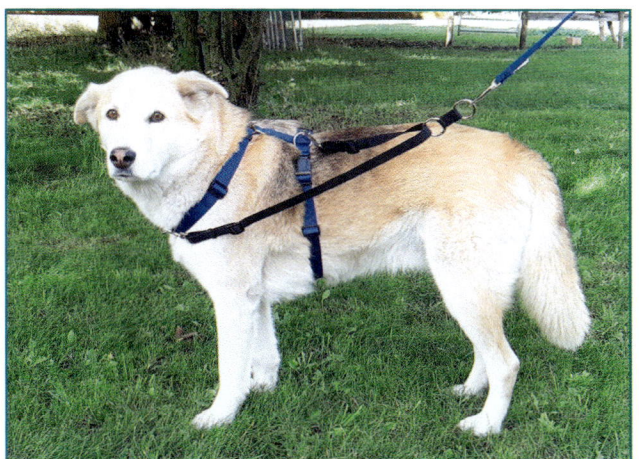

Ollie models the TTouch Connector in use with the TTouch Harmony Harness and leash/handle set. The Connector provides the dog with more space to sniff and explore their environment on leash while providing the benefits of Two Points of Contact.

The newest piece of equipment in the TTouch Tool box is the TTouch Connector, a short, piece of nylon with a light snap at each end. The original idea for this came from Finland. One of our Practitioners, Pia Arhio-Letho, liked the concept of the Harmony Leash with the sliding handle but she had four Border Terriers to walk at once. A friend of hers, Liisa Pennanen, who makes leashes and collars and came up with the solution. By shortening the leash and putting a ring in the middle she could one dog to each end of the leash, while allowing the sliding connection. This allowed her to walk four dogs using two leash and handles and still have two points of contact on each dog.

Robyn started using the concept in 2018 with very pulley dogs that needed a longer leash for more space. Typically a single point of contact is used with a long line. Unfortunately, when attached to only the front ring, the harness slides and pulls the dog out of balance laterally. When the line is only attached to the back ring, the pressure can create more forward pull in the dogs.

The TTouch Connector is an adjustable length of leash nylon with a snap at either end. It has a tab with a ring that slides along the nylon which divides the pressure between the front and back of the harness. You can attach a long line (leash) with a snap, use a rope, or the leash with the handle extended, attached to this sliding ring.

It is similar to using the Half-butterfly but easier for most people to manage and allows for multiple dogs to be lead in balance while with two points of contact.

The Connector can be adjusted to the individual size of the dog. With a short legged dog you have to experiment with the length so he isn't constantly stepping over the connector.

How to Use it:

The TTouch Connector can be used with any well fitted harness that has a chest ring and back ring. Snap one end of the Connector to the chest ring and the other to the back harness ring and attach your leash or rope to the sliding ring.

Adjust the length of the Connector so that it is short enough so that the dog will not step into it but enough slack to allow the connector to move from the one side of the dog to the other as the handler changes sides. You do not want to make it so long that the Connector really "folds" over the ring, negating the sliding effect and creating more pull. Adjusting the length can take some experimentation and use before you find the optimal length for your dog's height.

As you move with your dog allow them the space to sniff and come into their own balance. The beauty of the Connector is that you can give your dog the freedom to explore while maintaining the potential to encourage them back into balance as you have to direct them or change direction.

Walks should be enjoyable for dog and handler. The Connector makes it easy to allow for an enriching walk, sniffing, exploring and interacting with the environment safely.

The longer leash length allows you to let the lead slide when your dog pulls which interrupts the opposition reflex. Allow your dog some space and pause. As you are ready to redirect or bring the dog closer to you, simply stroke the lead as you step forward and come up to the side of the dog.

You can easily bring the lead forward to make a turn or stroke the lead 'up' as you step forward helping a dog to shift his weight back and come 'off the forehand' and come into balance. Many of the techniques described for use in conjunction with the Harmony Leash and Handle will be equally useful with the Connector.

As Robyn asks Harvey to stop in balance she steps forward as she strokes the leash upwards and slowly melts the leash contact down. This allows Harvey to stop with all four feet underneath his center of balance.

The Connector helps encourage mental enrichment and contained exploration when walking your dog. This 'freedom' helps reduce pulling and allows dogs' to walk in balance.

Part 5 ~ Dare to be Different

In most cases, working with dogs on leash has a fairly uniform "look", one handler with some sort of tether to the dog. For some dogs however, there are limitations to this common approach. Tellington TTouch works on a Feldenkrais principle that the nervous system pays more attention to something that is not habitual, ie unfamiliar or different.

When dogs have very ingrained habits in their behavior, whether it be balance or reactivity, one of the fastest ways to change this habit is to interrupt it with a very different, non-habitual experience.

Feldenkrais is a human based method, developed by Moshe Feldenkrais in the 1960's that suggests that the nervous system can learn in one lesson if there is no pain, fear of pain and if it is done in a non-habitual way. These principles are the basis for many of the Tellington TTouch Method leading exercises for all animals. To change a habit, we need to replace it with a more useful one by doing an exercise completely unfamiliar to our the and the subconscious. This is the principle behind many of our leading exercises using two handlers, since it asks the dogs to do an "easy" exercise that is completely unfamiliar—this requires the brain and nervous system to "pay attention". The article on the next page explains how 'habits' bypass the 'thinking' part of the brain. Offering 'novel' experiences helps access the thinking part of the brain to change habits.

Hint Hound

Playground for Higher Learning

All of these leading techniques can be very effective on their own however there is even more benefit to be gained by incorporating "The Playground For Higher Learning". ("See Getting in TTouch with Your Dog" by L Tellington-Jones).

"The Playground For Higher Learning" is essentially a variety of obstacles and surfaces that a handler asks a dog to mindfully navigate. Poles and cones are laid out in a range of patterns encouraging the dog to focus and pay attention to their balance, which in turn helps to promote self-confidence.

Using obstacles to encourage Loose Leash walking in an interesting and engaging way. Having concrete points on which to focus prevents aimless walking and unnecessary repetition. Asking the dog to work on and around obstacles, sometimes while bending their body through turns can be very helpful in teaching balance and helps to shift the dog back off of the front legs.

Central Pattern Generator

By Mary Warick

Central pattern generators are neural networks within the spines of mammals – including human beings. These neural networks are autonomous within the spinal cord, and once activated, do not require "supervision" from the brain. An "active" central pattern generator will drive rhythmic flexion and extension of the muscles involved, without requiring attention to sensory inputs to govern timing. Examples of such patterns are breathing, swallowing, walking, running, swimming, flying for birds, hopping for bunnies and wallabies, and scratching for dogs and cats. Some CPGs operate continuously, such as breathing; others are activated by the intention to perform a particular task, or behaviour. A CPG can have a portfolio of variations that modulate the pattern overall in response to sensory cues…for example, variation in walking on a level surface, uphill, and downhill – patterns of extension and flexion are different in part but overall rhythm is the same.

Once established, a CPG (including its variations) will be the default pattern that the movement will follow. To override or modify it, a new variation has to be "programmed". Supra spinal centers in the forebrain and the brainstem are necessary for initiating and controlling loco-motion. Areas in the cerebellum receive information from sensory receptors and apply it to intra and inter limb coordination – when they are paying attention. To create and establish a new variation requires that the brain "wakes up" and pays attention again.

This can be achieved through a couple of techniques. One technique is to initiate and re-peat a very small, unaccustomed movement that is a segment of a larger movement numerous times – either by instructing the subject to perform the movement, or by manipulating the limb – slowly, attentively, and with returns to a complete resting/inactive state between movements. An-other technique is to perform a movement, but put a constraint in place that will prevent some part of the "normal" pattern from being executed – thus modifying the pattern. A third is to take the subject through a completely unfamiliar movement, or series of movements – slowly and at-tentively. This holds the brain's "attention" long enough to have the new variation noted. With a variable amount of repetition for each and every unique individual, the new option will be ac-cepted and control will be passed back to the CPG.

If this re-patterning is "successful", there may be apparent changes in larger patterns of movement following the exercise, as the new "option" is incorporated.

Of course, this is all assuming that the new option is useful/non-threatening/pleasant for the subject – if not, there will be resistance and rejection! Unless you are subjugating said subject for some purpose – and that is why you don't want to read about the experiments that have been done to discover all of this!

Homing Pigeon Leading Exercises

The Tellington TTouch Method has its roots in the horse world resulting in a wide array of unusual and creative leading exercises developed for work with dogs. Homing Pigeon is a leading exercise, first developed for horses, that has a handler on both the left and right side, simultaneously. The name, Homing Pigeon, is used to describe a variety of leading positions which involve a handler on each side. Handlers are connected to the dog with leashes or one of the rope exercises described below.

Utilizing any leading position in the Homing Pigeon configuration quickly encourages a dog to focus, be in balance, maintain distance from the handler, and gives a new experience in working with different people. It also gives information to both sides of the body and brain, and teaches a dog to be led from both sides. It is useful with reactive dogs to give more of a buffer between other dogs. Homing Pigeon can also be a way to introduce dogs to children without them having be a primary handler.   Dogs with separation concerns can be gently introduced to feeling safer with different people while still being connected to their primary person.

Homing Pigeon with two fixed leads. It would be better if the handler on the dog's right side was further away to avoid the dog feeling claustrophobic.

Homing Pigeon Lead Configurations

- **Two fixed leads** - Leash connected to: Collar and/or Middle Harness Ring and Front/Back Harness Ring

- **One fixed lead and one sliding lead** (Fixed on front and back rings, sliding on middle ring)

- **Bee Line** (pg 54) (A rope threaded through the top ring or a swivel snap on the top harness ring)

- **Butterfly** (A rope is looped through the chest ring and back harness ring with a handler on either side)

One of the most challenging things can be giving a dog space. The more you can step away from your dog, the more likely it is that your dog will start to find his own balance.

Regardless of which configuration of Homing Pigeon you use, one of the most important things to remember is **COMMUNICATION**. If the two handlers are not communicating with one another and making a plan, the dog will be confused and not know what is being asked of them If you don't know where you are going, the dog won't either! . This exercise will help develop good communication and planning skills which will enhance your effectiveness when handling your dog on your own, improving clarity and self-awareness.

The Bee Line is one of the ways you can lead in a Homing Pigeon configuration.

Two leaders guide the dog on a sliding line. The absence of a fixed point on the lead gives the dog the opportunity to find their own pace and balance without being "micromanaged".

Handlers must use clear body language and intention to guide the dog. This makes handlers more accountable and improves communication in all leading positions.

This exercise helps increase self confidence in the dog and is an incredible tool for puppies who are learning to walk on leash, dogs who lag and have been dragged along on leash and dogs who have separation concerns with their humans.

Hint Hound

It's all about Communication!

Homing Pigeon leading configurations are wonderful exercises for dogs of all types and help create many different kinds of positive change but it's not just the dog who benefits. Handlers gain a lot from practicing leading with another person. Besides taking you out of your own habitual patterns of leading a dog, it also encourages you to be a better communicator!

In Homing Pigeon one person has to establish themselves as the "Captain", deciding where to go and when to do it. This means that you have to clearly tell your "co-pilot" what the plan is.

Having a clear plan is not just important for the other person in the equation; it also gives your dog much more concise and clear information, making it easier for them to appropriately respond to what you are asking.

Sometimes it can be useful to verbalize your plan even if you are leading a dog on your own. It will prevent you from aimlessly walking your dog and give yourself time to prepare for clear, effective signals.

Do your best to give the dog enough space and to look where you want to go, rather than staring at the dog.

Beeline

The Beeline, originally called the Clothes Line or Washing Line was developed at a workshop. Carol Rochaix-Wright and Susan Assad, TTouch students at the time, were working with a German Shepherd puppy during a shelter visit. The puppy had started to show collar and leash reactivity. They came up with the idea to put a harness on the puppy and simply run a piece of "clothesline" rope through the top ring on the harness and just follow the puppy where she wanted to go. We didn't see a remarkable change that day, although the puppy was moving on the lead and that was a change. We went back a day later and the shelter staff reported that the puppy was not reacting to the leash and collar the way she had. Hmmm. Very interesting. It seemed as though the unexpected experience changed the way the puppy felt about the constraint of the leash.

In the beginning, we primarily used Beeline with puppies, or any dog who was not leash trained, to help them feel comfortable on the leash. It allowed them freedom to feel safe, move in balance and be comfortable being on a lead without feeling too restricted. By giving a dog more choice, within parameters, it helps give them more confidence and in turn helps them learn to make better choices.

Since experimenting with the technique it has revealed itself to be an invaluable exercise for dogs who have separation concerns, are very nervous, pull on the leash, or lag on the leash. It is also a great exercise for handlers to give up micro-managing and reduce their own pulling habits.

In the Beeline handlers use a sliding rope to help guide the dog in a new and unfamiliar exercise that helps dogs find their own balance and prevents handlers from inadvertently pulling or micro-managing.

What is the Beeline?

The Beeline is a single rope running through the top ring on a harness with a person holding each end. The line should slide easily through the ring. Ideally a swivel ring is added to the top harness ring so the line won't tangle should the dog spin.

The rope should be a small enough gauge that it slides freely, but is easy to hold. The most important decision about the width of the rope is how easily it can slide through the harness ring.

For larger dogs, a soft, 10mm gauge rope is ideal, smaller dogs require 6mm or narrower. Try to find a soft, flexible rope material that is comfortable to hold.

The rope should be 4 - 6 metres (12 to 18 feet) in length.

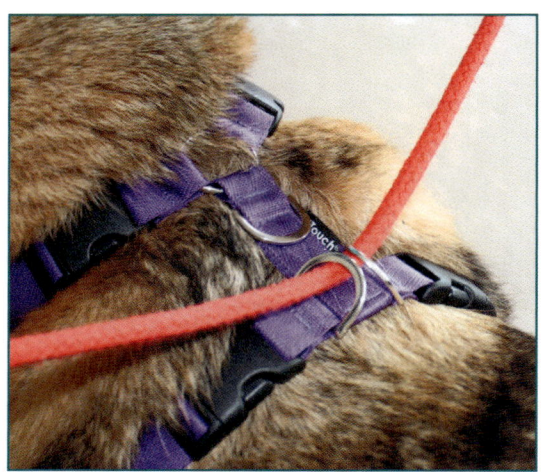

For basic Beeline, the line threads through the back ring on the harness.

Set-Up

Run a rope through the top ring of the harness; ideally through a strong (should be rated to the weight of the dog) swivel clip attached to the rings. Tie an overhand knot at both ends of the rope so that the line will be secured should one handler have to let go. Each handler holds the knotted end of the rope. Their outside hand should be at the knot, their inside hand supporting the line. Both hands should be palm up.

Adding a swivel to the back ring makes changes of directions or spinning, easier to navigate between handlers.

When to use it

Using the Beeline can be beneficial for: puppies, dogs with separation concerns, dogs who are reluctant to go on lead, dogs who freeze, are not leash trained, move slowly, are nervous, or for dogs who lean against the leash. Beeline is also useful for handlers who tend to "micro-manage" their dogs.

The leaders walk at a comfortable distance, guiding the dog with their body language and verbal cues. Since the line is not fixed, the Opposition Response is lessened and dogs will often come into balance very quickly. Do not be concerned if the dog crowds in one direction or the other, especially if they have separation concerns or are weary of strangers. Ignore this and continue engaging the dog with different obstacles, serpentines etc. and use of the Playground For Higher Learning. As the dog becomes more confident and balanced they will move more towards the middle of the line.

Starting Off

When beginning with this leading exercise it is very important to resist the urge to pull forward. Ideally the movement starts with the ropes in "supported slack",. Ideally there will be a little dip in the rope on either side of the dog; no pressure but not dragging.

The forward motion begins primarily with the body language and intention of the handlers. It is important that you allow the dog enough space. Do not crowd the dog, instead give him the time and space to process what is being asked.

You and your Beeline partner need to look where you want to go and think about having your bodies "open" in the direction you'd like to go, slowly shifting your weight to step forward then waiting for the dog to follow.

If the dog a little hesitant it is helpful to use an enthusiastic voice cue. If the dog is really stuck, pause, take your attention off of the dog, exhale, and perhaps try a few TTouches. At this point you may see a weight shift in the dog, indicating that they will be able to move off when you ask again.

In the freedom of the Beeline, this dog is moving towards his 'person'. Offering this "autonomy" within the parameter of the Beeline helps enhance confident and usually results in the dog choosing to find the middle within a few sessions.   Ideally the handlers would be looking where they want to go but this is a difficult habit to overcome. Looking where you want to go, rather than at the dog, helps create more clear, less intense body language and posture.

Turning with the Beeline

One of the biggest challenges with the Beeline is the feeling of not having control – think of having 'influence' instead of control. The position of your body is key.

Ideally there should be a bit of "supported slack: in the rope on either side of the dog.

Turning is done mostly through your body position – the person on the outside of the turn steps forward with the rope, even if you are behind the dog slide your inside hand forward and over the dog's shoulders.

The person on the inside of the turn should rotate their body and look where they want to go – be sure there is no tension on the inside of the turn.

The outside handler may lift their hand to the mid line of the dog to help indicate the turn.

Notice that Robyn (in blue) steps ahead slightly through the turn.

The inside handler must override the instinct to pull on the line. Pressure on the inside line will actually send the dog in the opposite direction than desired.

Robyn's hand helps guide the turn from the outside, even though Ollie finds it a bit perplexing why these humans are asking him to walk in a circle in the living room.

Stopping with the Beeline

If the dog is very forward there are several useful techniques to help the handlers get forward so they can effectively ask the dog to stop.

The **Stroke and Stride** technique. Stroke the rope, hand under hand, as you keep moving forward along side of the dog. Both handlers think about "stretching" the line sideways. This brings the line to a neutral position, straight out to the sides rather than pulling backwards. This makes it is easier for the dog to stop in balance

You may add a **Quarter Turn** to stop where the handlers make a quarter turn towards the dog as they **Stretch and Melt** on the line.

Stretch and Melt: Both handlers "stretch" the line out to the side, meeting resistance, as they keep their feet moving, melting the stretch into a stop.

Tandem Reverse: Both handler simply turn around, change your hands on the rope and start walking in the opposite direction while verbally engaging the dog. This technique works especially well with puppies and only when the rope is threaded through a swivel.

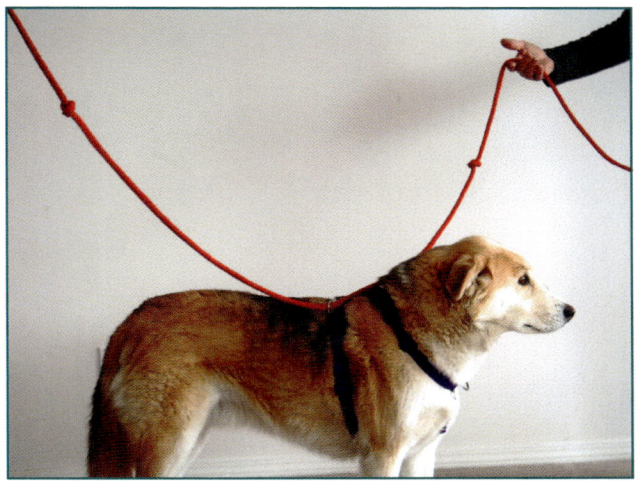

Serpentine: If a dog gets ahead, utilize turns. The worst thing you can do is walk in a straight line. Bending lines help bring dogs into balance and helps the handlers get out of the Water Ski position.

Variations

1 Tie a knot in the rope on one or both sides of the dog – about two-three feet from each side. This sets a parameter for how much a dog can move between either handler.

2 Run the single rope through the front ring on the harness. This technique may be helpful for dogs who are habitually falling forward and unable to shift their balance back over their feet.

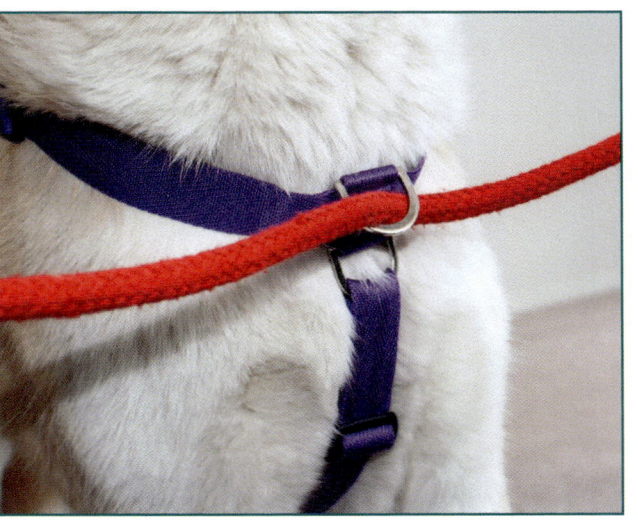

Slide the Line

The Sliding Line is a helpful technique that can be used in a variety of ways.

The moving action of the line creates a dynamic connection to the dog, instead of a fixed one, and helps subdue the Opposition Response. It is usually used as part of a Homing Pigeon leading exercise, but a Sliding Line can be used in a pinch with one handler when you do not have a handle or double ended leash.

Have a partner hold a collar or harness in their hands; they will act as the "dog". Thread a rope line through one of the rings and hold one line in each hand. Have your "dog" start to move away from you. As you ask the "dog" to come back to you; slowly rotate your body left and right allowing your arms and hands to go with the movement. You will essentially create a gentle back and forth motion to redirect the "dog" without pulling back.

Contrast how this feels to pulling and releasing, using a "check" motion, or just walking the other way. Most people in the "dog" role experience that the Sliding Motion is very soothing and almost compels them to come back to the handler, even if they "try" to pull.

The Devil's in the Details

One of the most important keys to success with any of these exercises is how we use our bodies or position ourselves while handling the dog.

Many of us take some details for granted such as how we hold the line, where we stand in relation to the dog and where we look. In reality it will be these small details that make the difference between a graceful partnership between you and your dog and floundering. This is especially true when working with more complicated dogs.

In most cases, holding the leash with your palm up, rather than the more common palm down, will encourage you to use fine motor control rather than gross motor control and reduce reflexive pulling on your part.

Being aware of your position level or slightly ahead of the dog's shoulder will go a long way in terms of interrupting any Opposition Response

Keeping your eyes soft and looking where you are going helps encourage breathing and makes your body language clearer for the dog.

The Beeline is easiest when combined with the Playground For Higher Learning.

 The obstacles allow for clear intention on the handlers part and encourage the dog to move in bending lines which helps promote better physical balance and flexibility.

 It is important to look where you want to go rather than stare at the dog. Staring at the dog is a strong habit for most people.

Beeline is an excellent exercise for puppies. Here these handlers are "Meeting" as they as for a stop. The "Melt" would happen in the next frame.   Ideally they will keep their feet moving until they are standing straight across from the dog's neck. This will prevent them from becoming "water skiers".

Butterfly

This configuration is a halfway point between the freedom of the Bee Line and the specific influence of Two Points of Contact. The sliding nature of the rope reduces any inadvertent pulling on the handler's part and the contact on the chest helps dogs shift their balance back. The Butterfly offers a choice rather than a command and gives more information about what the handler wants than the Bee Line while still allowing the dog a choice about where they are in relation to the handler.

In the Butterfly, Lori and Dennis use a Quarter Turn and are "Meeting" then "Melting" to ask Cassie to stop.

Getting Started

While your dog is wearing a harness, take a 15 to 20 foot rope and thread one end through the back harness ring. Take the other end and thread it through the chest ring, tying the ends of the rope together. Take care that the knot in the rope does not impede the rope from sliding through the harness rings.

Adjust the rope, now in a large loop, so that each handler has an even amount of rope. Use a soft rope, cotton is ideal.

When to use it

The Butterfly can be very effective with dogs who are very forward, dogs who lack confidence, and dogs who are very habituated to one handler.

It is not always easy to do with very small dogs or small puppies. Their smaller stature may cause the front rope to come up near their face.

How to do it

The rope can be held in two hands, with one on either side of the knot or add a handle for one handed use.

The ropes should ideally be in a straight line from the shoulders with a little slack in both ropes on both sides, the handlers across from each other. Move forward without pulling on the ropes, keep your hands softly open. Like all Homing Pigeon exercises, the more you can stay level or ahead of the dog, the better you will help the dog walk in balance and self-carriage.

Turning

When turning with the Butterfly, imagine the wings of an airplane. The person on the outside moves forward – you can take your hands forward to avoid pulling back. The person on the outside of the turn may find it helpful to move their hands towards the dog's shoulder to indicate the turn and the inside person rotates their body and looks where they want to go without pulling.

Using the Handle

Adding a handle to the Butterfly leading exercise is a fantastic way to improve lightness and create more ease for the handlers.

Depending on the length of the rope you may be able to hold the handle with the inside hand and guide the handle over the outside of the turn to indicate direction and then step away from the dog to avoid crowding the dog.

If the rope is too long you can hold the handle in the outside hand and use your inside hand as a 'guide' to keep the rope from dragging. Avoid closing your hand around the rope. To turn from this position use your handle to act as an anchor near your body so you can slide your inside hand away from the Handle to indicate the turn.

Stopping

Like virtually all Tellington TTouch leading positions, the Quarter Turn is a very effective technique to use with the Butterfly when signaling a dog to stop.

As you want to stop, keep your feet moving as you make a Quarter Turn of your body, towards the dog. Both handlers think about "stretching" the rope straight out to the side. This can be done with or without the addition of the Handles.

If you do not have the Handles you may have to add "Stroke and Stride" to avoid the dreaded "water ski" position. As you signal for a stop, keep your feet moving and stroke the chest rope as you Quarter Turn, melting as your dog stops. This helps keep you level with the dog's ear and neutralizes any backwards pressure on the leash.

Robyn and Mandy use a Quarter Turn and "Meet and Melt" to ask Ollie to stop. Notice how Ollie has stopped in balance with a leg at each corner and his weight over the middle of his body.

Half Butterfly

The Half Butterfly is the cousin of the Butterfly. Exactly as it sounds, the Half Butterfly is essentially the Butterfly leading position with a single handler. The Half Butterfly stabilizes the harness and prevents any lateral movement. It is not generally a Homing Pigeon exercise since it has one leader although it can be used, a bit like the Dragon Fly - see page 53.

The lead length gives you ample room to allow the rope to slide some distance, especially helpful with large, pulley dogs. Allowing the slide breaks up the Opposition Response so the dog has nothing to pull against, and comes back into balance.

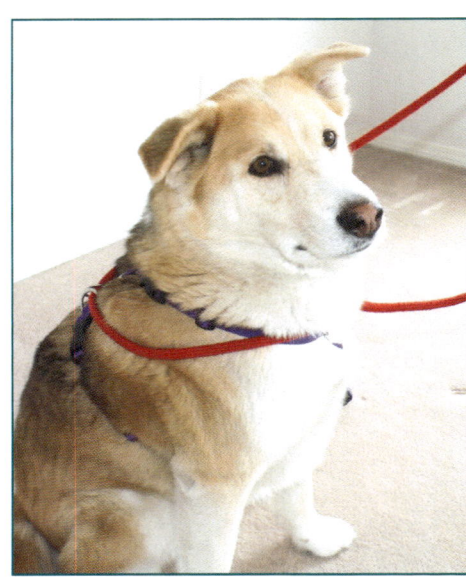

In Half Butterfly the line threads around the far shoulder, through the chest and back rings.

Getting Started

Take a 16 to 20 foot rope, threading one end through the back harness ring and center the rope. Take the other end and thread it through the chest ring, tying the ends of the rope together. Now the handler has contact that is unfixed, providing a dynamic, sliding motion.

Use a soft rope, cotton is ideal. If you only have access to nylon rope, please wear gloves.

When to use it

The Half Butterfly is a good option when you are alone and want to give a strong dog more space or to work with a second person when coaching a client.

How to use it

Hold the knotted end in your outside hand with your index fingers between the two ropes. Slide up the rope with your other hand, also with the index finger between the ropes. This is where you can use stroking the ropes to steady your dog. If the dog pulls, let the rope slide through the hand closest to the dog, followed with a underhand stroke of your other hand. The slide interrupts the opposition so the dog doesn't have anything to lean against.

The Butterfly allows the handler to help the dog shift their balance back without having a fixed line to trigger an Opposition Response.

ADVANCED EXERCISE – DRAGONFLY

 The Dragon Fly is an excellent exercise for dogs that have become extremely habituated to moving while out of balance, leaning forward while walking, or outright pulling. This exercise looks similar to ground driving a horse but with a handler at the dog's head as well.

 The front handler (or handlers if in Homing Pigeon) walks the dog on Two Points of Contact, at the chest and the back ring. The front driving line (rope) threads around the chest of the dog and along either side of their ribcage. The handler with the chest line rope walks behind the dog holding the ends of the rope in one hand and the other hand further up the lines with a forefinger between the two lines.

 Several years ago in England I had a lovely German Shepherd who was very anxious when asked to walk beside someone on a leash. He was very strong, pulled hard and would get stressed and jump up on his person. Off leash he could manage to stay with her as long as he had a ball or something as a distracter. I thought it might help if we could give him the experience of walking on a loose leash with all four feet on the ground.

We used a harness and ran a driving line through one of the side rings, across his chest through the harness and back through the other side rings so that both ends were behind the dog.

With the dog in Homing Pigeon the intention was that the handlers in front stayed at the dog's head and only guided to make turns. The front handlers NEVER pulled back on their leads. We did two sessions with this dog and the change was quite amazing. He could walk on the leash with much less concern and seemed to be more aware of his surroundings in a calm fashion.

How it is done

 Working from behind, the driving lines influences the dog's speed and overall balance. The driving lines are held with the palm up and the index finger in between the two lines. Use a stroking motion to slow the dog down. As you reach up the lines with the right hand, allow the right shoulder to follow to help keep from bracing through your hips or back and stay in neutral.   As your right hand slides towards your body, reach up with your left hand/shoulder and repeat the sliding towards your body motion with your left hand. It is this technique that avoids the "sled dog" response.

When you ask the dog to stop be sure to avoid the leaning back with your shoulders behind your hips, keep your upper body neutral and hips softened. "Meet" the contact to signal a stop and then very, very slowly melt (rather than release, or let go) so the dog can come back into balance as he stops.

Uses of the chest line

- Leash pulling – especially if the dogs are severe pullers

- Dogs nervous of things behind them

- Shy dogs – be sure to give them enough room behind

- Dogs that jump up on people

- Dog and handler that need the experience of walking with a loose leash

Things to remember

- Great in conjunction with Homing Pigeon but not required
- It is most important that the handlers do not give a backward signal on the leads at the front of the dog.
- If dog leaps on people then using the Butterfly configuration of Homing Pigeon helps keep the dog more balanced.
- The person behind the dog is meant to regulate the speed, using stroking to slow, and only ask for stop with "Meet and Melt", never a steady pull.

Part 6 ~ Equipment Hacks

While a well fitted harness, double ended leash and handle are the ideal, we know that there are times that these will simply not be at your disposal.

The Balance Leash, and its variations are great examples of creating a technique to rebalance a dog with only the most basic equipment. Many of the Tellington TTouch techniques have been developed while working with shelters and rescues, where equipment choices may be limited. As a result there are many simple and clever ways to make effective, balance and posture friendly

Ropes

Rope harnesses are fantastic tools for use in shelter or rescue situations or if you ever find yourself having to contain a loose dog. All you need to create a custom fit harness is a light weight rope between 12 and 18 feet long. The length varies depending on the size of the dog and what you plan to ask of them while wearing the harness, but there is some wiggle room and the versatility means that you can make a wide variety of lengths work.

Simple Rope Harness

The Simple Rope Harness is quick and easy to put on and take off, making it a great technique to remember, especially in shelter and rescue situations.

Getting Started

1. Find the middle of the rope and tie an overhand knot, making a loop just large enough to slide two sections of rope through. Hold the knot in your hand, palm up, with your fingers separating the two ends of the rope.

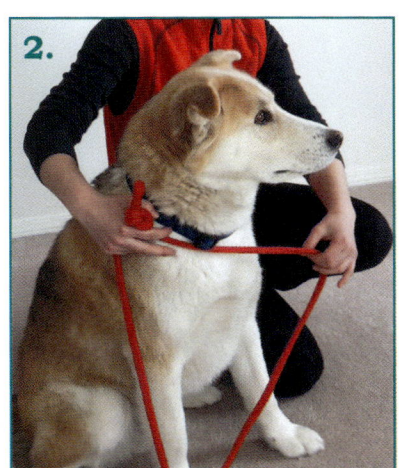

2. With the dog standing next to you, drop both ends of the rope on the opposite side from you.

With your free hand, bring one end of the rope around the dog's chest .

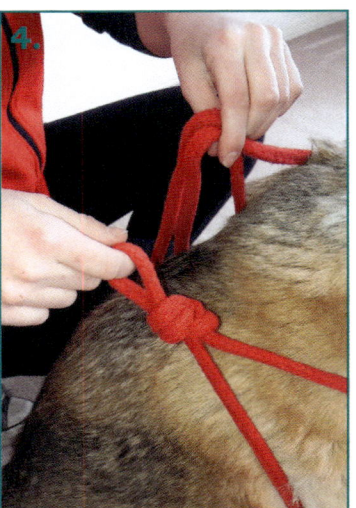

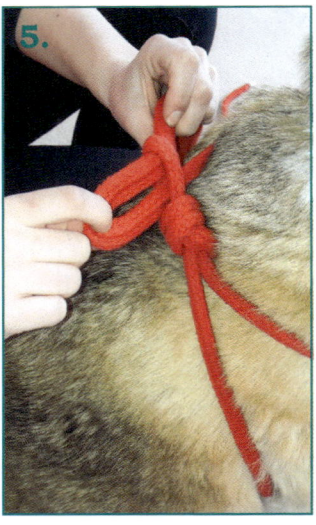

3. Take the other end of the rope under the belly, just behind the elbow.

4 & 5. Bring the two rope ends together and adjust the length so they are fitting snugly around the dog. The knot should be sitting between the dog's shoulders on top of the back.

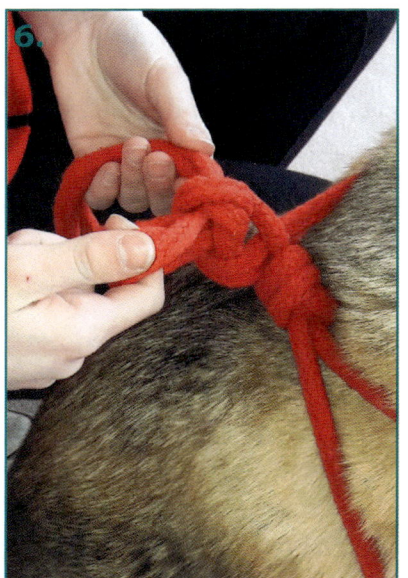

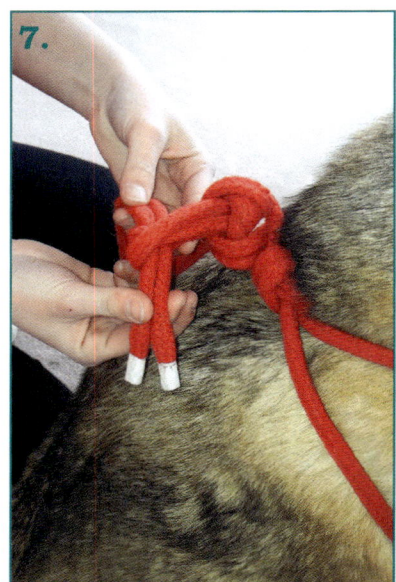

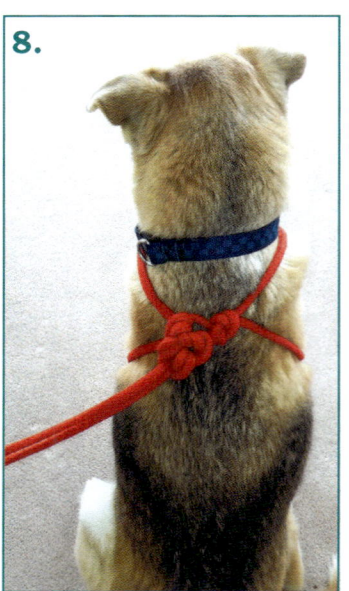

6 & 7. Once you have adjusted the sizing, fold the rope ends and feed them through the knot loop just enough to daisy chain it several times before pulling the end through to "lock" the rope. This keeps the rope from tightening and gives you a "leash".

8. To undo the Simple Rope Harness, simply "unchain" the rope once and allow the rope to unfurl.

When to use it

It is very useful if you find a dog running loose and you only have a rope, moving dogs in a shelter or kennel situation when you have a lot of dogs of different sizes (adjustable sizing), introducing harnesses to a puppy or re-educating dogs who are harness shy. This is a great option because you do not need to slide anything over the dog's head or touch their feet.

Troubleshooting

Once you are comfortable with this technique you can adjust it to be used on nervous dogs who may not appreciate close human contact. This is ideal for use in shelters and rescues.

Try the "Necklace" configuration (see photo), where the dog actually steps into the rope harness so that the handler does not need to reach underneath the belly.

Once the dog steps into the "Necklace" the adjustment steps are the same as with the regular Simple Rope Harness as described in steps 4 through 8 on the previous page.

With a little practice, this harness can be placed on a dog in seconds while giving the dog enough space to feel safe and secure.

Balance Rope Harness

The Balance Rope Harness gives more leading influence than the Simple Rope Harness and makes contact lower on the chest which helps create balance over all four feet.

It allows the handler to give separate signals from two points of contact – the top of each shoulder. This is useful for dogs who pull sideways or those who tend to be clingy. It is also helpful with dogs who freeze or sit down.

This configuration can be modified to be used in a Butterfly (page 58) leading position, complete with handles.

Getting Started—The Original

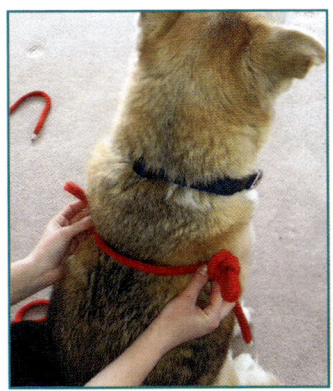

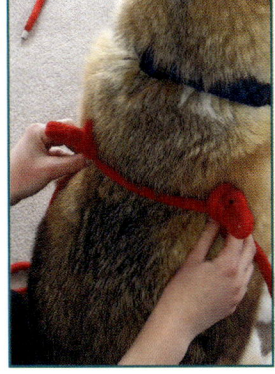

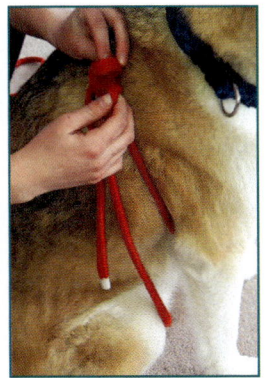

1. Fold the rope in half, in approximately the center of the rope tie an overhand knot.

2. Place the knot over the top of one of the dog's scapula to measure.

3. Tie a second overhand knot to sit approximately over the other scapula.

4. Take one end under the belly and fold a loop through the knot loop.

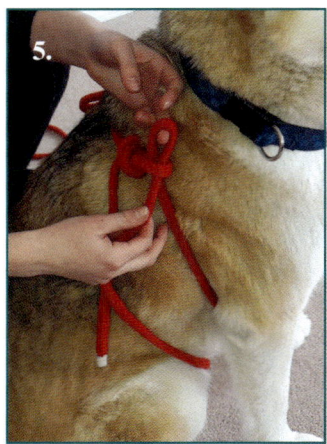 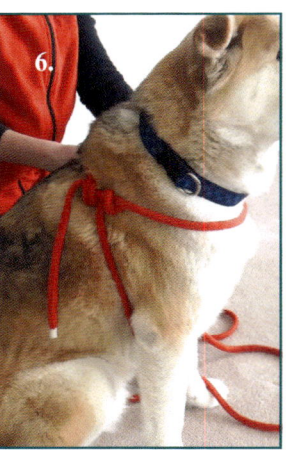 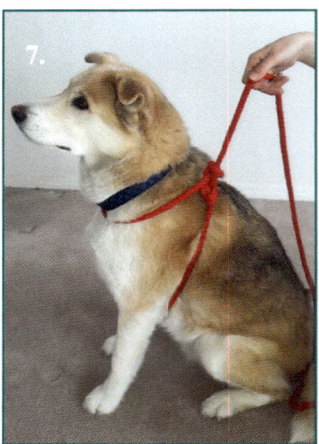 

5. Pull the rope all the way through the loop to secure the rope end into a knot.

6. Bring the other end of the rope across the chest and fold through the opposite knot.

7. Pull the rope through to the end to secure the knot.

8. You should now have a secure rope harness with two lengths of rope coming from the top.

When to use it

The Original Balance Rope Harness can be very useful for guiding puppies. It allows you to give guidance from either side and help dogs understand leading signals. It takes a lot of pressure off the neck.

Getting Started—Balance Rope Handle Butterfly Harness

The Balance Rope Harness if very versatile. With a small modification it can be used with two handlers in the "Butterfly "leading position. Handles, when available can be added to make this even more effective as an exercise to rebalance "on the forehand", "pull-y" dogs.

 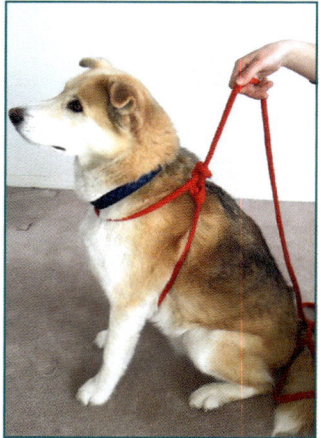 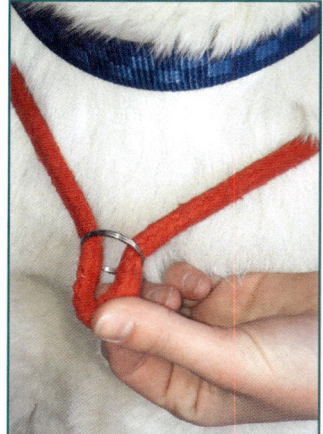 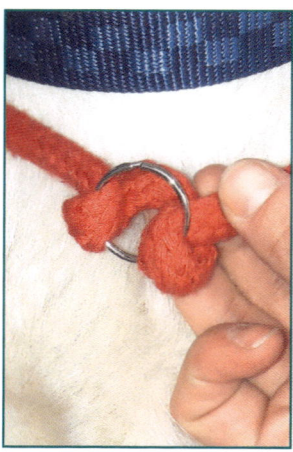

1. Make the initial knot approximately 12 inches from one end or the rope.

2. Continue the steps from above until you have secured the harness.

3. Take a ring and fold the center of the chest rope through.

4. Take the fold back and up.

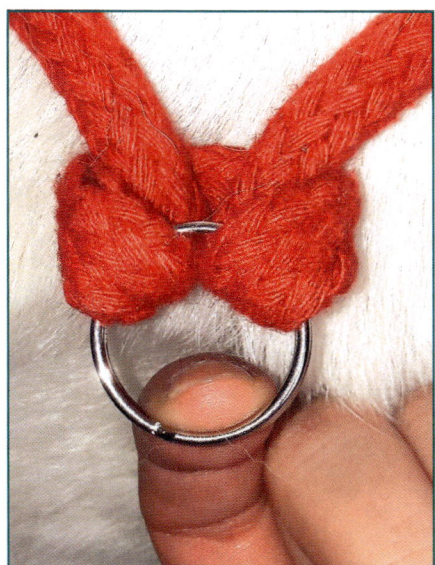

5. Lock the fold up and onto itself.

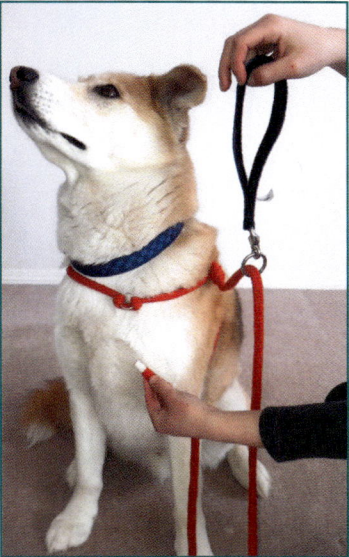

6. Take the long end of the rope and thread it through the handle, if available.

7. Thread the rope through the front loop on the chest. This will secure the ring to the harness.

8. Take the rope through a second handle, if available.

9. Tie the long rope to the shorter end of the rope at the shoulder and carry on with your leading exercises!

Karabiners

Small, lightweight karabiners are a great piece equipment to keep on hand. For most dogs the inexpensive types, not rated for rock climbing, are strong enough.

They can be used to modify harnesses with small rings to allow the rope to better slide on the front or top ring for Bee line or Butterfly.

You can also use it to modify a harness that does not have a front ring attachment so that they can be used with Two Points of Contact.

With a little creativity and a short loop of rope, Karabiners can also be used to create a sliding "handle-like" imposter when attached to a dog collar.

Metal Rings

Lightweight metal rings, such as heavy duty key chain rings are also very handy hacks. The can be folded into a rope (as described on page 58) to make a front point of contact.

Since ring quality and strength vary so much, it is very important to consider the size of dog and how many pounds of pressure they could potentially exert when used in an exercise.

Swivel Snaps

If available, swivel snaps are a fantastic addition to the Beeline.

Using a lightweight swivel snap on the back of the harness ring prevents handlers from having to reorganize or untangle a line should the dog spin or weave suddenly.

As with the metal rings, quality and strength varies so be sure to use a swivel that is appropriately strong for the dog it will be used with.

If you are not sure of the swivel's strength do not use it as the only means of containment or you might unexpectedly end up with a loose dog!

Start these exercises in an secure enclosure or indoor space.

An important consideration for creating long lasting, positive changes for your animal is how you conduct your early lessons. You can use all the exercises, equipment and self-awareness in the world, but if you are working in a distracting or over stimulating environment in the first attempts, progress will be limited. Like most areas of dog behavior and training, management is incredibly important for changing habits and promoting socially agreeable behaviours.

When you are first practicing balanced and aware Loose Leash walking, it is very helpful for you and your dog to do so with as few distractions as possible. Creating a calm, focused environment during the first few sessions will make it easier to establish new patterns of balance. Once these new patterns have been integrated for you and your dog, you will find it easier to cope with, and regroup from less than ideal situations.

Using elements, like the Playground for Higher Learning (see Getting in TTouch with Your Dog by Linda Tellington-Jones) is also very helpful for creating positive changes in a dog's balance and helps expedite the learning process. If you do not have access to obstacles be mindful not to walk in too many straight lines. Using curved, looping lines is very effective in rebalancing and containing a dog's forward motion. Remember that bending lines helps to shift a dog's weight off of their front legs and better enable them to maintain good balance and focus.

Using different surfaces is part of the "Playground for Higher Learning". It enhances dogs confidence and promotes better posture by encouraging a relaxed neck and back.

If possible, plan your sessions during a naturally relaxed time of day, not right before a meal or after a dog has been cooped up for an extended period of time. It is also useful to work in an area that is familiar to your dog or a place where your dog has had a chance to sniff and explore off leash or at least with as little handler interference as possible.

It is well known that staying hydrated is important for people especially when they are learning. We have found the same to be true for dogs. It is essential to keep water accessible to your dog whenever he is in a learning session. When you offer the water, wait a few moments to see if he will drink. This also provides a useful "pause" for your dog when information and learning can be assimilated.

Sessions should be kept short and sweet. Ideally sessions are not so long that your dog is mentally over stimulated. Working in new postures and with new habits is deceptively fatiguing mentally and sometimes emotionally too.   Think about finding success in moments, not minutes. At the beginning it is important to recognize that changes will be small. If you have ever tried to change an ingrained habit in yourself, you know that it is easier said than done. Be happy for small changes or short periods of change. A long-term habit will not usually disappear over night. Mindfulness and awareness are the first major hurdles when working to shift habits.

   Learning new things requires the nervous system to pay a lot of attention and is much more difficult than doing something familiar or habitual. If your dog suddenly starts to find really interesting things to sniff, starts to pant, get really "itchy" or shuts down and flops on the ground, you have done just a little too much. Don't fret if you let the session get to this point. Simply pause, breath and end with a few TTouches. (See Pigeon moments - page 63)

   If your dog (or a dog you are working with) has separation concerns, from you or their person or other dogs, make the sessions easier at first by keeping them near their friends. When a being does not feel safe it is almost impossible to learn. As the exercise becomes more familiar it will be easier to address the separation concerns. In some cases, successfully learning new skills and becoming more balanced will create more self-confidence and lessen the anxiety surrounding separation indirectly.

   A common way to positively promote Loose Leash walking, is the use of treats and food as a reward and/or distraction – whether used with the Clicker or otherwise. Food is an incredibly powerful motivator and can be used successfully with any of the exercises and equipment discussed in

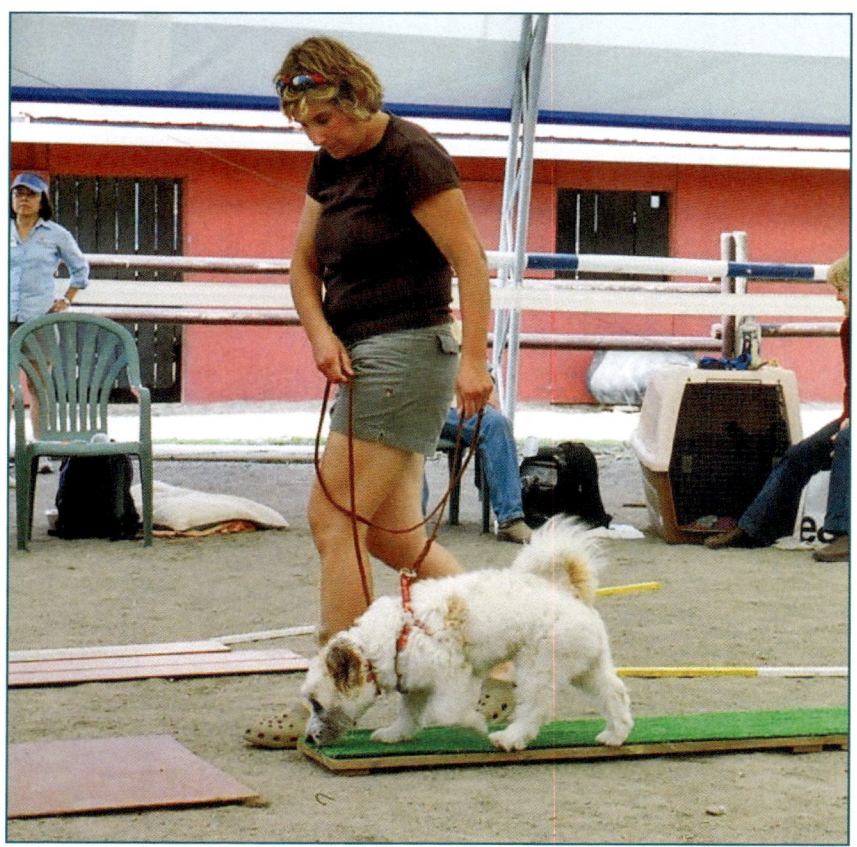

this book. The beauty of TTouch is that it can be seamlessly integrated into most positive training protocols.

   As with any training tool, food should be used with discretion. Some dogs can become so distracted by food that they do not actually pay attention to their surroundings or how they are moving.

PIGEON MOMENTS   By Sarah Fisher

I call them 'pigeon moments' purely because we have pigeons here at Tilley Farm and I have witnessed many occasions when a dog started staring at the pigeons when we were working with them in the indoor arena or outside. Whilst it may seem as though a bird or something else in the environment might be the cause of distractions for dogs it can lead you down the wrong path if you inadvertently overlook important details when interacting with your canine clients/friends. Over the past few days I have had the privilege of teaching students in the UK and in Austria about the importance of looking for small clues. We were able to identify several 'pigeon moments' that had nothing to do with the environment but were linked directly to what we were doing at the time.

TTouch is not just a quiet way of connecting with animals with our hands. It is an integrated approach to handling and furthering the education of animals through observations of body posture, coat patterns, nervous system responses and body sensitivity, use of ground work exercises aimed at improving balance and co-ordination, use of equipment such as the TTouch harness, and assisting the handler to modify or change their own habits to help the animal move beyond their own habitual responses. The focus of how I teach this work is looking for the smallest threads that weave together to create the more obvious picture.

One aspect of the quiet connections I make with my hands is to highlight any area of sensitivity in the body that may trigger a 'pigeon moment' when I handle any dog. As I build the trust and start stroking the dog slowly on his chest, around his shoulders and gradually extend the areas I am touching (over several sessions if necessary) I feel for the quality of the coat and the mobility of the skin and watch and feel for even the most subtle of responses and shifts in the dog's posture, rate of respiration, blinking rate and so on. I also pay close attention to any 'pigeon moments' that might occur.

Some of the dogs I have been working with over the past few days were so clear in their responses it was as though I had flicked a switch. One dog was sensitive around the base of his right ear, another at the top of his left hind leg. Each time I quietly touched the dogs on these tight or sensitive areas they either stared at another dog or looked out of the window even though there was nothing there. As soon as I moved my hand and gently touched the dogs on different parts of their bodies the dogs were able to re-engage once more.

Slowing everything down makes these moments stand out. Moments that could be so easily overlooked. Every student could clearly see that these responses were triggered by my hand contact on these small areas of the dogs' bodies and were not directly related to the environment in any way. We also observed that one dog only had the 'pigeon moment' when tension on the lead increased. As the guardian learnt new ways to handle the lead and help the dog to move in balance all the 'distractions' magically seemed to 'disappear'.

Gathering this vital data helps us identify how we can utilize our skills and time to help the animals in our care. It can also highlight areas that may warrant further veterinary attention as I meet many dogs that have discomfort in the body but still lead what appears to be a very active life. On numerous occasions it was the observation of these 'pigeon moments' that enabled guardians to recognize that their dogs, or client dogs, only became 'distracted' when touched on specific parts of the body, when asked to turn in a particular direction, sit or maintain a stand and so on; veterinary investigations revealed skeletal changes or damage to soft tissue that required pain relief and/or modifications to the management of those dogs.

Next time you notice a dog looking away or shifting his focus from what you are asking him to do, ask yourself he is really distracted or did he actually dis-engage, and why? What happened in the moments before the 'pigeon moment' and how were you interacting with him at the time? Avoid jumping to conclusions based on one observation. Gather all the information possible to ensure you really are on the right track.

Pay close attention to how he sleeps, how he sits and stands, the coat patterns, his general posture, the position of his ears and tail, and his response to slow, gentle contact with your hand. Build the picture and strive to be the best dog detective possible as you look for all the clues held within the glorious body of your dog. Begin to question whether it is our interactions that are triggering some of the dog's behaviours we wish to modify or change; always remember the nervous system never lies.

Part 8 ~ Harness Choice

Today there are so many choices of harnesses that choosing one for your dog can be overwhelming. There is nothing that works for all dogs and all situations, however, there are some harnesses that tend to be more versatile than others and have more fitting options.

When choosing a harness, keep in mind what kind of leading configuration you want to use, your dog's conformation and any considerations for your individual dog's concerns, (ie are they head shy or paw shy?). At the end of the day, your dog's comfort needs to be one of your primary concerns.

In our opinion practically any harness is more humane than leading a pulley dog on a collar, or more aversive device. Today there is some debate about the potential damage done to dog's shoulders with front attached models which must be considered. From the TTouch perspective leading with Two Points of Contact, as discussed previously, reduces the amount of stress on the shoulders and set dogs up to be more successful on leash.

In the first edition we included the pros and cons of various harnesses we have used. This section has been eliminated because of the growing number of harnesses on the market that could work with the techniques described in this book, as long as they have a front and back attachment.

With so many options on today's market, choosing the best harness for your dog can be overwhelming.

Part 9 ~ Head Collars

Our use of canine head collars has changed over the years. When we first started the Tellington TTouch for dogs they were a frequently used tool to help influence dogs' behaviour and balance. With the development of more effective harnesses we rarely use head collars for regular handling. **Today our use of head collars is usually limited to dogs that are reactive, generally for short periods of time; or with a person who is not physically able to handle their dog.**

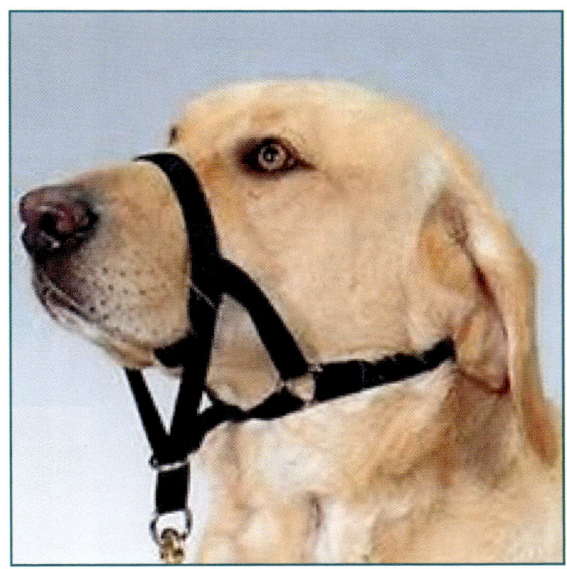

One concern with using head collars is the potential for damage to the neck and also that they inhibited a dog's ability to look at scary situations and to display calming signals. Head Collars used on their own are ineffective to help dog's find good balance and posture.

When we do use head collars they are ALWAYS used with Two Points of Contact – one on the head collar (with a light snap) and the other either on a flat collar or ideally with a harness. Without the second leash attachment you have no way to steady, balance or direct a dog smoothly; your only option is to pull or release and most people pull. Pulling a dog's head to the side may cause damage to the neck, twist him through the body and over develop one shoulder.

As with many aspects of Tellington TTouch we have a step-by-step process to introduce a head collar and the process can be 'chunked down' into tiny steps when necessary. These steps can also be used to introduce a muzzle.

Some dogs are not initially comfortable wearing a head collar. They will try to rub it off, walking with their noses to the ground or will be so distracted by it that they cannot focus on what is being asked of them while others simply freeze and shut down.

The TTouch Method for introducing and using the head collar can help to avoid these difficulties. This process is the same regardless of the brand or design of head collar you use. There are many different kinds on the market - which is wonderful considering that dogs' heads come in many shapes, and one brand by no means fits all!

Introducing the head collar

If at any time in the process the dog shows concern, pause and find a way to "chunk it down" and make the steps smaller and easier. This might mean taking a break, going back a step, using some treats or changing some aspect of the process. The usual steps to introduce the dog to a halter are as follows:

Circular TTouches are done all over the dog's face where the halter will lie, and the dog's response to these TTouches is observed. If he has trouble being handled around the muzzle you can explore touching with the back of the hand or using a sheepskin or other soft material.

Mindful, TTouch Mouth work can be very helpful in helping dog in preparation for wearing a head collar.

A light elastic (face wrap) or Calming band, is put loosely in a figure eight over his muzzle, crossing under his jaw, and tied loosely at the back of his neck. He wears this while doing things that are pleasant, usually for only short periods, but several times if that is necessary.

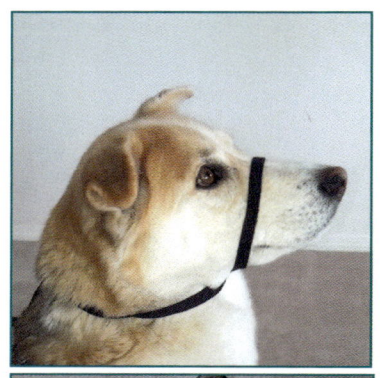

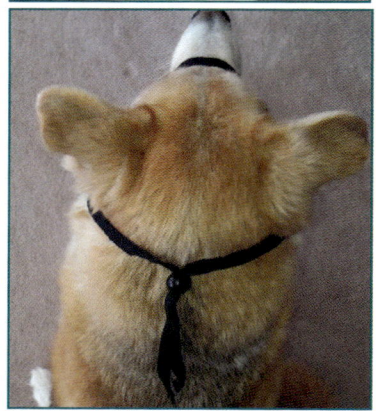

A Face Wrap, made from an elastic bandage or sewing elastic for small dogs, can be an excellent step when introducing the feeling of wearing a head collar. A toggle makes sizing

Fitting the head collar

The head collar is fitted so that the dog can open his jaw wide enough to yawn -without coming against any pressure of the material or rings. If using a Halti® brand this means being able to put, from the back, both thumbs at the same time on the inside of the head collar where the nosepiece is stitched to meet the jowl having the thumbnails not touch the jaw. This manner of fitting may seem heretical to many, and some of the reasons for allowing it to fit loosely are:

We always use Two Points of Contact - one on a flat collar or harness, the other at the head collar. It is preferable to use a double-ended leash, with a lightweight snap for the halter. This removes the need for a tight-fitting halter that is necessary if there is no other connection with the dog.

Many dogs who seem to "dislike" the head collar will suddenly accept it once it has been loosened so it is very important to be mindful of fit.

With a leash on the collar, the head collar is then fitted -loosely - over the elastic. It seems to make the process easier for the dog if the elastic is left on to begin with. Without adding the weight of a leash the halter is again left on while having fun - or eating a meal or being given treats. The dog should not run loose or be left unattended during this time.

When the leash is first connected, it is not used at all. The added weight of the leash is a change that the dog needs to become accustomed to before any signals are given. You will find as the handler that it takes quite a bit of awareness to maintain a loose leash!

If having the leash connected to the head collar is difficult for the dog, an intermediate and sometimes very successful step, can be added: Remove the halter and fasten the leash to the face wrap where it crosses beneath the jaw. This is much more acceptable for some dogs, and can help them to get used to the weight of the leash.

The process described above may take longer than "just doing it", but will make it easier for dogs who are having difficulties. With many dogs one can go speedily from step to step, but breaking it down allows you to see more clearly where it may not be comfortable for the dog.

At each of these steps you can add the clicker – if you are using clicker training, or just a few treats to make it a positive experience. For some dogs playing with a toy at this stage can also help the process be more positive.

Using the head collar

The TTouch technique of using the halter is also a little different from other methods. One aspect to keep in mind is that it is used to "influence" the dog by showing the dog what is expected of him, rather than being used for the purpose of "control", which implies prevention of some behaviour. In order to influence the dog easily, it is important for the handler to stay at the dog's head, rather than falling behind to a position where they can "correct", but not "direct".

All the signals are in the form of "Meet and Melt"(pg 9). When we take the time to watch how animals respond, it is evident that most of the time they react on the release rather than while the signal is being given. This observation makes it clear that it takes a moment for understanding the leash request to be transformed into action. We might need to re-think the snappy responses we often ask from dogs, and look at what happens to the dog's balance and demeanor when we give sharp and sudden commands.

The signal to come forward is ideally done using the voice and no contact on the leash. If you need to give a signal it should be on the collar or the harness. If the dog is pulled forward by the halter, the tendency is for the head to rise which causes the back to drop - making it harder for the dog to step forward under himself.

Similarly, the signal to turn, "Meet and Melt' is made by showing the dog which way to turn his head, while asking for the "forward" off the flat collar or harness., or just your voice. If the turn signal is to be clear, the signal from the halter leash needs to come from the front and to the side-rather than behind, or behind and to the side as so commonly happens if we are standing behind the dog's shoulder. It becomes really easy for them to learn to turn their heads if the first few times we have a treat for them in the hand holding the head collar leash.

When stopping, the principal signal is given on the flat collar or harness and the halter is used for fine-tuning. A benefit of the double connection is that if the dog pulls on one, the pressure on it can be released, and the contact picked up on the other. Allowing the dog moments of falling forward as you switch from one to the other leash makes him have to catch his balance. If you keep taking away what he is leaning against he stops leaning! You will find that you will be able to use a light signal in this manner – even with very strong dogs.

Why use a head collar?

Halters are not our 'go to' piece of equipment, nor do we use them on many dogs, however they do have a place in the tool box.

Head collars helps to teach dogs to deflect their gaze when they may be provoking antagonistic behaviour in other dogs. This communication signal should ideally be taught with a verbal request such as saying the dog's name, and not pulling on the dog's head.

It provides the handler with a sense of security with a dog who exhibits unwanted reactivity. When the handler feels more secure they can think more clearly and be a better teacher for their dog. He in turn can gain confidence from a leader who demonstrates that they knows what they are doing.

Head collars are also useful for small or physically compromised handlers who become better able to contain and redirect large, strong dogs.

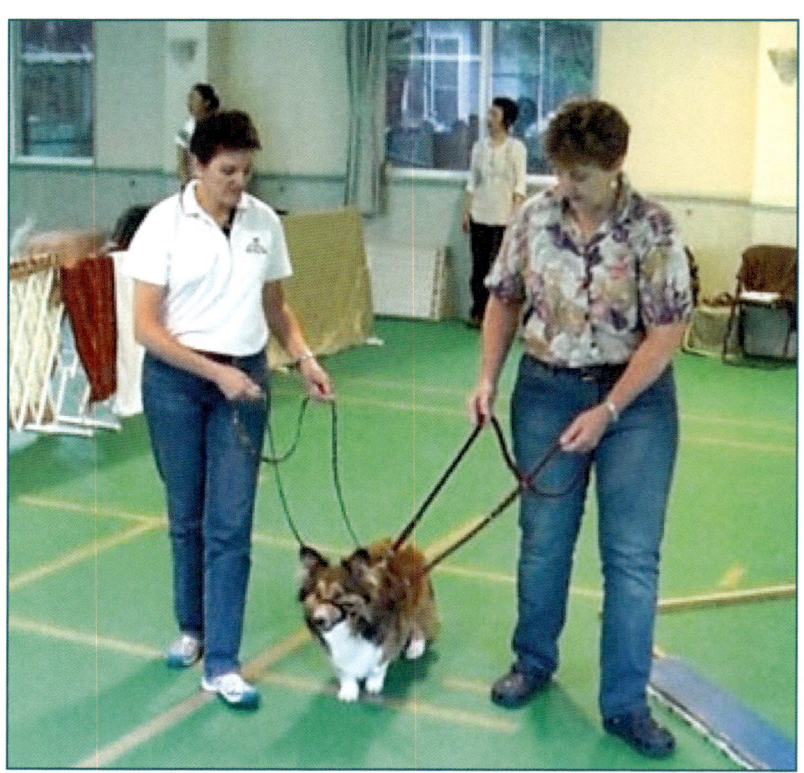

When using a head collar in a Homing Pigeon leading position only one handler has points of connection to the head.

Part 10 ~ The End of the Leash

It was our decision to put our dogs on lead so it should be our responsibility to intelligently and compassionately help our dogs become balanced and confident during that time. Changing the discourse and placing the onus on the handler actually gives you more options and potential for creating change.

When a dog is reactive or is not responsive on leash, it is important to look past the symptom and see what is at the root of their behaviour. From a Tellington TTouch perspective we know that it can all come down to balance, and in turn confidence, or lack thereof. After reading through this text, I hope you are aware that interrupting the Opposition Response is the easiest and most effective way to change the way most dogs behave on leash.

Becoming more responsible for how we act or react and becoming more aware of what we do is well within our control and gives us better choices when faced with a challenging situation. The exercises and techniques outlined in this book are designed to empower you with a set of tools to give you choices so you can help yourself and help your dog.

Using the tools and techniques described in this booklet will hopefully make life much easier for handlers and dogs so that we look forward to hearing "my dog likes to walk on a loose leash" !

Contributors

The expression "It takes a village" has been embodied by the evolution of the Tellington TTouch Method. From its inception in the horse world, Linda's work has expanded and progressed to span a multitude of continents and species. We would like to thank the following people for the direct or indirect, contribution towards this book and its concepts and techniques:

Linda Tellington-Jones; for her unwavering ability to see the perfection in every animal and being and the development of this unparalleled way of working with animals.

Sarah Fisher; for her observational genius and the development of Leash Stroking, the Sliding line and the original TTouch Harness design. We so appreciate the addition of "Pigeon Moments" in this book.

Peggy Cummings; the extent to which Connected Riding has inspired and refined our work with dogs and their handlers has been extraordinary.

Carol Rochaix-Wright & Susan Assad; for their "thinking outside the box" and creation of the Clothesline, now known as the Beeline.

Hannah Wilkinson; her idea of using handles with the Butterfly has been a fantastic addition.

Janet Finlay; for the wonderful article, "Why Use a Harness".

Peter Dobias DVM; his tireless pursuit for dog's wellbeing is so appreciated as is his permission to include his article "One Jerk Can Cause A Lot of Damage".

Mary Werick; for her fantastic explanation of "Central Pattern Generator".

There are bound to be others whom we have inadvertently missed but we do so appreciate the collaborative nature of the work and love the way that it is ever evolving through our collective experiences.

We would also like to thank our army of proofreaders and sounding boards who helped beyond measure; Philip Pretty, Christine Schwartz, Lindy Dekker, Lauren Mc Call, and Debby Potts.

Photos Credits:

Bob Atkins for Charles & Gordon Publishing
Valeria Bossier
Eugenie Chopin
Sarah Fisher
Robyn Hood
Annalena Kuhn (Cover)
Mathilde Krog Larsen
Lauren McCall
Indra McMorran
Judy Mori
Amanda Pretty
Andy Robertson
Christine Schwartz

Printed in Poland
by Amazon Fulfillment
Poland Sp. z o.o., Wrocław